how girls thrive

how
girls
thrive

JoAnn Deak, Ph.D.
with Dory Adams

Revised And Expanded Edition

ISBN: 978-0-9845787-0-2

Contents

Acknowledgments

How Girls Thrive was written while I was an administrator at Laurel School in Shaker Heights, Ohio. There are many at that great institution who deserve praise and thanks:

- Barbara Barnes, head of school in the 1970s and 1980s: She managed to get me interested in independent schools and in girls' schools. She hired me as the first in-house psychologist at Laurel School.

- Leah Rhys, head after Barbara Barnes: She is a woman before her time and pushed us to do a study with Carol Gilligan and her team at Harvard.

- The board of trustees who approved my taking time off to complete the first edition in 1998.

- Ann Klotz, the new head of Laurel who continues the tradition of excellence. I love her mantra to the girls: "Walk with grace and purpose, and in doing so, use your gifts on behalf of others."

For those in positions of power and influence at the National Association of Schools (NAIS) in 1998 go special thanks. The first edition was published by NAIS, distributed free to all of the independent schools in the country in that year, and promoted in their bookstore until the final printing just over a year ago.

Dory Adams was the Director of Career Paths and Gender Equity Services. She was the initiator, the catalyst, the editor, and the driver of the first edition.

The present board of NAIS returned the copyright to me so that I can get this into the hands of this generation of educators and parents, or, as I like to call them, neurosculptors of our next generation.

The actual launch of this edition is taking place at the National Coalition of Girls Schools conference in New Orleans in June 2010. Whitney Ransome and Meg Moulton, previous co-directors of NCGS, created an organization that changed the world for girls and girl's schools. Suzanne Beck, the current director, continues the monumental work of supporting all those schools whose special mission it is to help insure that future generations of girls continue to have a single-sex setting as an extraordinary educational choice.

I'd like to thank all of the girl's organizations in this country that continue to work so that girls continue to thrive. These include such great organizations as the Girl Scouts, Girls Inc., Power Play, Write Girl, Girls Can Do, PACE, and Tarrant County Challenge.

I would be remiss if I didn't mention all the wisdom and research I have collected in my work with schools, parent groups, and organizations around the world. They are just too numerous to mention. There is a partial list on my website, but it is ever changing and growing. I would especially like to thank those wise and experienced female heads of school that have devoted twenty, thirty and forty years to the growing of girls. I don't want to miss any, so there is no specific list here. But, you know who you are and how you have shaped my thoughts and ideas through the years.

And finally, to the hundreds of girls (and boys) and parents who have shared their thoughts, hopes, dreams and fears with me. The education was worth so much more than any Ph.D.!

— JoAnn Deak

I came home from the first day of the first grade in tears. I had not, as I believed I would, learned to read that day. Eventually, I was given the magic "decoder," and I have been crazy about reading ever since. JoAnn Deak has given me the long-dreamed-of opportunity of having my name on a book. She has been a delightful, challenging, and always inspiring author to work with. My certainty that her work is changing the world for girls made it all the more special for me to be a part of this project.

Our volunteer readers gave me an extra boost of energy with their positive comments when the end still seemed too far away. Seth Wilschutz offered a calm, technologically savvy shoulder to lean on when I panicked over PDFs and the like. Theo Coonrod, a goddess of grammar, stepped in and with her "English teacher eyes" saved me from multiple embarrassments (effect/affect, need I say more?). Any remaining errors are, of course, all my own.

It's not possible to work on a book about girls for parents and educators without thinking about the ones I have known. I am inspired continually by three of the best mothers I know, Carol, Cathy, and Leah, and their thriving daughters, Tara, Maddie, and Olivia.

As for educators? Well, Steve Clem has mastered the art of the "teaching question." Barbara Stock taught me the importance of getting out from "behind the scenes," and constantly modeled what feminine success looked like. Sue Thompson knows how to open the door, but stand back and let me go through on my own. I am grateful to them all, and so many more.

— Dory Adams

Foreword

This well-written book instructs with stories from professional experiences. It sparkles from conceptual clarity. JoAnn Deak begins with a no-nonsense summary of research on gender issues. This is an enormous and complex area, and her coverage is easy to read and useful. She then offers us good original thinking on the much-muddied concept of self-esteem. Her ideas are both theoretical and practical and are presented in ways that have implications for actions. In fact, one of the best things about this book is its recommendations for immediate practical steps in our school systems.

JoAnn Deak is an earnest idealist and a rigorous researcher and critic. She's a good combination of head and heart, of school administrator and writer. I recommend this book to all educators (and even parents) who want to improve the world for girls.

— Mary Pipher
Lincoln, Nebraska

Why This Book Now?

It's been twelve years since the first edition of *How Girls Thrive* was published.

We (my spectacular editor, Dory, and I) have worked hard to make this edition current, better, and more relevant. I'm often asked, "In a nutshell, what has changed, what are the issues?" True confession: I'm not very good at nutshells. Topics about human beings are just too complicated to fit in a nutshell.

Which is why every chapter and every topic has new parts added that reflect recent research and current issues and topics faced by girls. So, bits of the answer appear on almost every page, or I'd rather envision them not as bits, but as pearls. I hope that, after you have completed the whole book, you will have a string of pearls!

However, there is one trend that it is troubling enough for me to want to address it here and now. In the last twelve years I have worked with thousands of girls (and boys) in schools across this country and many others. As I look back and try to remove myself far enough so that the lens I'm using sees major patterns, there is one that emerges that causes me pause — stress.

Stress isn't new, nor is it necessarily bad. In fact, our neurobiology was designed to handle stress. When faced with conflict or challenge, the chemical system of adrenaline and corticoids combine with an effusion of neurotransmitters to prepare the brain and body to respond with an extremely "souped up" system. Therefore, stress can be, and is, motivating, and as such is a natural and necessary part of life.

So why does this stress pattern that I am seeing cause concern? Because stress is incredibly painful, debilitating and downright dangerous if it is pervasive and continues over long periods of time, especially if there is no perceived light at the end of the tunnel.

An example of this destructive side of stress is the suicide, recently in the news, of a teenage girl who hanged herself after a long bout of what was called bullying. Just like stress, bullies have been around for a long time, or at least my grandfather said there were bullies when he went to school, and that was over a century ago. So what has changed?

Bullying, The Media and Social Networking: The Trifecta of Skyrocketing Stress for Tweens and Teens

There is an excellent, comprehensive article, "Big Bad Bully," in the September 1995 issue of *Psychology Today* (best found at www.psychologytoday.com/basics/bullying along with a slew of related articles) that covers bullying in an exceptionally comprehensive way, including the what, why, when, how, who and what to do about it. So I am not going to try to do that again here. My point is that bullying has reached a level of insidious pervasiveness that puts many adolescents at risk. And, in terms of mental health and self-esteem issues, girls are especially vulnerable.

My work and my books focus mostly on the positive view of how to "grow" healthy and resilient human beings. Indeed, throughout *How Girls Thrive* — from the brain research to understanding external and internal constraints, through a true understanding of self-esteem and how to build it over time, as well as grasping the significance of crucible events and crucible moments — the message of this book is how to ensure that girls will thrive even in the face of the toxicity that they are facing, and will face, no matter what we do as caring parents and educators.

I am not prone to ringing the danger bell. But to answer that question about what has changed for girls causes me to do just that. What's different, why the alarm? When I was a teen, if a friend was upset with me, she could say negative things about me to others and/or to me. I would, at the least, be able to go home and have some sanctuary. Also, unjustified meanness (compared to justified, when someone does or says something to deserve a negative response) was seen as bad or not nice. The few really "mean" kids were marginalized and had no real social power. Enter two *huge* changes: social networking and the media.

On one internet site alone thirteen social networking sites are listed. Each can be accessed by one click and each sends out messages to thousands of members. You can see how fast and easy it has become to make bullying viral.

Social networking has now removed all sanctuary. With emailing, IMing, tweeting, texting, blogging, Facebook, and new outlets all the time — there is no escape. The onslaught can be and often is twenty-four/seven. Not only is it never-ending, cyberspace spreads the harsh word (or devastating picture) to thousands of teens in a few seconds and *the effects cannot be erased* by "just kidding" (JK), or "I'm sorry."

How pervasive is social networking and its effects? The Pew Research Center reports that

- The number of teens engaged in daily text messaging has jumped rapidly from 38% in 2008 to 54% in 2009 and is still climbing.

- Frequency of texting has overtaken every other common form of daily interaction with friends with face-to-face communication accounting for only 33% of interactions.

- Teen girls ages 14-17 average more than any other group at 100 or more messages a day (more than 3,000 texts a month).

- One in three girls report being bullied/harassed through phone calls and texting

Other studies report that

- Teens say they tweet 5-10 people before deciding what to wear to school.

- Most teens say they are fearful about what might be posted about them on-line.

- One in four teens report knowing someone who has had a bad experience because of information posted on the internet (ranging from having "sext" forwarded around school to being sexually victimized).

- Many teens report that their parents are "clueless" about their cyber-activities, and 40% say they don't tell their parents what they are doing on-line.

We know from the research on stress, that the ability to cope is reliant on both periods of respite and the ability to take control and do something about what is happening. You can see how both of these requisites have been almost totally removed by the tech world.

The media provides a "double whammy." Television, movies, magazines and music all support and encourage put-downs. Whether it is rapping or reality TV, it has become socially acceptable, no, worse, *popular* or "in" to denigrate others for no justifiable cause. What has been considered abnormal behavior has now become the norm. I'm not trying to sound old or not with it, but rather to provide the perspective of someone who has watched over and thought about girls for her entire professional life.

A prime example of how "in" it is to be mean, is the recent and rapid growth in the popularity of Formspring. Formspring is a kind of cyber bulletin board where messages can not only be seen by the 28 million people who visit it each month, but can also simultaneously be sent to anyone's Twitter, email or Facebook account. The key here is that, unlike some other sites, the writer is anonymous.

So, I can say that someone is a _____ (fill in the blank). Or that Susie's boobs are too small for any boy to ever look at her. The end result is that a child's peers can take dead aim and not be seen as the shooter. Not surprisingly, Formspring has been linked to the recent suicide of a 17-year-old girl.

This is a critical issue of basic safety and sanctuary. Teens tell me all the time that being respectful and kind is considered "geeky." They are afraid to be supportive of others and not play the game of teasing and bullying others. The fear is palpable in most girls with whom I have spoken, whether individually, or in groups. They wax poetic (frighteningly so) about how they are afraid to step an inch out of the social expectations because they may then be the recipient of teasing and harassment and, the onslaught of public and social networking which will cause the erosion of their social standing, indeed, of their very selves. This social tidal wave is more than frightening to those of us trying to build a world that promotes the healthy and strong development of the next generation.

It is important to know that the girls themselves want help. Children and teens tell me that they appreciate parents who set limits on their networking, schools that cover topics like bullying in their life skills classes, the teachers who will not allow any type of teasing or meanness in their classes, or visiting the homes of friends who have parents present and set a climate of social safety.

I'm not saying that we should remove all social stress from the lives of children. In fact, many of my workshops cover just the opposite: the normalcy and need for children to experience a wide variety of friends and the conflict that relationships always bring to the table. We are not born socially savvy animals; experiencing conflict and learning how to deal with it are part of the path that leads to that extraordinarily important skill. In fact, new brain research is showing a part of the brain (the anterior cingulate cortex) that is activated when we experience conflict and make mistakes. It seems that when the ACC is activated, it increases the probability that whatever is happening will be remembered, thus ensuring real learning and growth from the experience.

Stress is needed and leads to better learning; conflict is needed and leads to social expertise. In a nutshell (well, I guess I can do it sometimes!), the load is too great. Bullying is everywhere, it is inescapable, the cost has skyrocketed and there is often no respite. Counselors who work with junior and senior high school girls find that no matter how much a girl is being hurt by the messages in Facebook's Honesty Box, or at Formspring — even when they are vile, denigrating, and/or sexually explicit — she is unable to stop looking at them, often returning again and again.

Added to the stress of threatened or real bullying in a child's world there is the pressure to be successful, do well in school, look great, and join athletic teams and clubs, and many of our children are staggering under the load. Bullying and social stress is one of the areas we need to lighten to make the stress of life more manageable.

Girls bring some additional cards to the table. In this book, you will find evidence that supports the assertion that females are even more prone to the costs of social conflict because of their neurobiology. The combination of their emotional system and that wonderful hormone oxytocin (see Chapter Three) predispose many girls to care deeply about relationships and, their connectedness in a group or school, and to give more weight to how other people view them. It is certainly a human characteristic, and boys care about these things too, but girls have an additional neurobiological dose (so to speak) of concern.

The numbers bear this out. Again, according to the Pew Research Center

- Girls average 80 text messages a day, while boys typically send and receive 30 a day.
- 59% of girls text several times a day to "just say hello and chat," compared to 42% of boys.

- 84% of girls have long text exchanges on personal matters; 67% of boys do.

But that isn't all there is to the story. When faced with confrontation, most boys most of the time, react with anger and project their distress outward. Anger is what we call one of the most positive of the negative emotions because it promotes immediate action. Boys usually get rid of their upset immediately (if it festers for a long period of time we have Columbine). Girls report that anger is not their primary emotion in the face of bullying. It is fear, anxiety or emotional hurt. These emotions tend to go inward and, as you will see in Chapter Three, begin the serious erosion of self-esteem.

My work in the area of bullying has brought to light another concern. Articles and experts are quick to point out the obvious costs to the victim and the observers of bullying. Their pain resonates with everyone as we think about it. But bullying, over time, changes the one doing the bullying and erodes that person's self esteem as well. I've been in the business long enough to see the pattern of long-term effects on bullies. They grow up not liking themselves. That not liking can lead to a lifetime of mental health problems like depression or suicide, or, head in the other direction: serious anger management, abusive behavior, and criminal actions.

Even though this book stresses change over time, I am well aware that for anyone who is in the middle of trying to help a girl (whether the bully or the bullied), long term is not enough. Again, the literature (especially, see Psychology Today website) has lists for everyone. Here are a few key approaches (pearls):

- Girls can practice the type of responses to general bullying that tend to stop a bully in his/her tracks. Fighting back is not one of them! Things like, "Hey, I thought we were friends, I would never do/say that to you." There is more of a list in what I would call the "avoid being a victim" literature.

- All girls (and boys) should have conflict management training.

- Make sure your girl knows she has an adult who will listen and help her cope with any social stresses she may face. (See the green blanket story in Chapter Four.)

- Be proactive. Bullying will happen in all schools at some time, so form a good partnership between family and school so that as a team you can deal with bullying issues (either head on or in a more behind the scenes way) before they get out of hand.

- When you see unjustified meanness, make it visible and make it clear that it is not "teasing" and not healthy and that it can't be part of this family, this class, this school, etc.

- **Critically important: Every parent should have their children's on-line account codes and check the postings at least once a month to help their children handle what is toxic, to set guidelines and limits, and to keep the conversation going about life in the cyber century.**

This serious point needs to be made: *no one benefits from bullying or unjustified meanness and everyone pays both short term and long term costs.* It is such a serious social cancer that we all need to intervene to reduce it. That is what this book is all about — a preventive and powerfully long lasting approach. How do we go about it?

First and foremost, we must help design and orchestrate environments (at home and at school) that lead to the layering, over time, of strong, resilient human beings with integrity — those who can better withstand bullying when it occurs, will not join in when it occurs, will do something about it when it occurs, and will not bully others. Although the focus in this book is on girls, the general principles are not that different for boys.

And when you need your own "green blanket" to help handle this thorny problem, write to me and I'll answer.

JoAnn
jdeak@deakgroup.com
www.DEAKgroup.com

Preface

"If I waited for perfection…I would never write a word."
— Margaret Atwood

Since the original publication of *How Girls Thrive* in 1998, the field of educational and psychological research has focused more on female development than ever before. Some attribute the beginning of the attention to Myra Sadker's and Nancy Frazier's work in the 1960s which culminated in their 1973 book, *Sexism and Society*. Other works followed, but it was Carol Gilligan and her study of adolescent females that penetrated the popular press and seemed to be the wake-up call for researchers to study seriously the development of females. Gilligan's book, *In a Different Voice*, became one of Harvard University's most popular publications. From that point on, work in gender research, theory, and opinion has grown at a remarkable rate.

The Gender Pendulum

Gilligan's work made it clear that, prior to the last few decades, the study of human development was really the study of male development. It was only a natural swing of the pendulum, then, that caused research to be skewed, at least in terms of volume, in the direction of the female gender in the 1980s and 1990s — to compensate for the dearth of work in this area prior to this time. Now, if you look at the popular press and media specials, there seems to be somewhat of a backlash: writing about the development and needs of boys has the edge. Perhaps in the near future the pendulum will settle somewhere in the middle, with equitable focus on females and males. In fact, I believe it is utterly necessary.

A review of the literature provides strong evidence that there is not an equal playing field in our schools, for females OR males. Clear data still shows that advanced math and sciences have a higher proportion of males than females in most of our high schools. However, there is dominating evidence that, on average, girls' grades and standardized achievement scores are significantly higher than those of boys. One outcome, for instance, is that this has resulted in an imbalance of females being accepted into competitive universities. Therefore, many universities are now struggling with finding ways of keeping numerical balance by gender in their student populations.

As you can see, I've been leading you down the garden path to this conclusion: This book is not designed to make the case that pervasive gender inequity for girls exists. The real need now, expressed by school personnel and families, is to figure out what we can do to facilitate effective learning and positive growth equitably for girls and boys. Both sexes need to be understood, leading to the design of environments that are as positive and effective as possible for both sexes. The scope of this book, though, is limited to about half of that population: the girl component of the equation.

Next Steps

When it comes to sex and gender equity, there still remains a critical gap between what we profess and what occurs. Schools, families and organizations need a clear way of looking at their culture, structure, and practices as they combine to help form a human being called a girl.

For instance, although administrators and teachers are becoming more aware of gender issues (one state, South Carolina, requires all districts to provide some form of single-sex education to meet this goal), there still appears to be a great deal of confusion about what the next steps should be. Some of the pertinent questions are:

- How does a school analyze gender equity with enough specificity to allow it to set priorities for action?

- If this can be done, how do you move to selecting those strategies, in a comprehensive way that will meet the differing needs of girls and boys?

- Is this piecemeal approach of selecting splinter techniques really going to effect systemic change in the institution?

- What happens if some teachers apply gender-fair techniques and others do not?

Once those holistic and specific assessments are completed, we need a way of evaluating what practices and programs match the needs to the most effective changes. This book is designed to help on both accounts.

Chapter Layout

While this book is at times directed at teachers and school administrators, it is intended also for parents and caregivers (who, after all, are key educators in the lives of their children). This is especially true of the last two chapters — where the advice, based on the best of current research — will go a long way in helping parents and caregivers bring out the best in each and every girl.

- Chapter One provides the reader with the foundation of literature that delineates the issues of sex and gender — to remind us of where we came from and where we need to go — it is designed to organize the massive amount of data (especially that of the last decade), into a brief, manageable summary.

- Chapter Two sharpens the focus and delineates the external and internal obstacles to girls succeeding in schools and in life. Having done that, it will become clear that the thorniest impediment to equity and quality of life (other than the basic human needs for food, shelter, etc.) for females is low self-esteem.

- Chapter Three is devoted to an in-depth analysis of self-esteem. This concept (often misunderstood or simplified in popular literature) needs to be understood clearly before attempting to change an environment or to influence the humans in that environment. In a way, it is at the heart of all our efforts to help girls become happy and effective.

- Chapter Four extends this notion of building the self-esteem of girls by looking at what I call "crucible events" and "crucible moments" in the lives of girls. How we respond to girls in these moments and during these events can go a long way in strengthening or diminishing their self-esteem.

Caveats

At this point, some caveats are in order. Of necessity, there will be generalizations made which are meant to convey trends that can be inferred from the literature in this field. It is also clear that there are exceptions to these general statements. However, it would be a mistake to reject a meaningful trend because you think of an exception to it. As my grandmother used to say, "Don't throw out the baby with the bath water!"

Many of the conclusions and recommendations are based on a weaving together of many studies and branches of research and literature. Therefore, you will not always see one study or one researcher's name attached to any topic.

Let Us Begin

My hope is that this book will help schools, organizations and parents begin the process of change — and continue working until we have transformed our world into more effective growing environments for children.

So, with that thought, let us begin.

CHAPTER 1

Gender Research and Theory — What Does It Say?

"Don't confuse me with the facts." — Connie Francis

If you go to the library and complete a computer search with the key words gender, female, education, development, pedagogy, or any combination of the above, you will be left with a staggering bibliography. You also will note a trend: the quantity of writing has increased almost geometrically each year since 1982 when Carol Gilligan's seminal work was published in her book *In a Different Voice*. One way of organizing this massive amount of gender literature in an efficient manner is to condense it into major themes or categories. For our purposes, the framework will be:

    I.   Physiological Research and Literature
         A. Developmental
         B. Hormonal
         C. Cognitive
   II. Psychological Research and Literature
         A. Self-Esteem
         B. Values/Morality
         C. Affect
  III. Educational Research and Literature
         A. School Structure
         B. Classroom Structure
         C. Curriculum
         D. Pedagogy

This chapter summarizes each area and makes connections to our work as adults in the lives of girls. Please keep in mind, as with all other areas of thought, there is no truth — only perception, opinion, judgment, and common sense. I'll try to add some objective clarity by relying on valid research as much as possible. Ultimately, however, each summary will present the material and conclusions from the standpoint of what a "reasonable person" would conclude after reading all of this stuff.

Physiological Research and Literature

Developmental

Through adolescence, girls mature faster than boys in areas traditionally related to school. Much of the developmental literature is based on observation and/or theory. For example,

- First-grade teachers know that, in general, boys' auditory discrimination of short vowel sounds develops at a later age than that skill in girls.

- Research supports this (in an indirect way) with the data that indicates that approximately 80% of remedial reading students are boys.

- A kindergarten teacher in an all-boys' school will move into reading-related activities according to a different time-line and will use different techniques than a kindergarten teacher in an all-girls' classroom.

- The literature supports the position that boys with summer birthdays are more at risk for academic problems than girls with summer birthdays.

- Parents and caregivers notice that boys seem to need to move more than girls or that girls seem to be able to sit still for longer periods of time.

Some of the more recent research focusing on neurobiological factors correlates to these observed differences in growth time-lines by sex.

Hormonal

Research on hormonal influences on the brain and resultant behavior is becoming clearer each year. Male and female hormones have a direct impact on the architecture of the brain and, therefore, on rational thinking and emotions:

- A simple summary of this vast body of data is that estrogen and testosterone, both in utero and throughout life, have a significant differential effect on humans. A prolific researcher in this field, Doreen Kimura at the University of Ontario, has a book on this topic titled *Sex and Cognition*.

- Much current work is being done to show the hormonal effects as they pertain to thinking and to behavior. Although far from definitive, this research supports that hormonal input of testosterone and estrogen influence structural and functional neurological differences by sex.

  An example is the so-called CAH (congenital adrenal hyperplasia) girls studied at the Chicago Medical School. These are females who received more testosterone in their systems in utero than a control group of sisters. The CAH females had measurable hormonal differences that correlated with concomitant differences in behavior and thinking patterns and skills: CAH females play more sports, play with more action-oriented toys, and show a higher level of competence in spatial skills than their estrogen normal sisters. These behaviors are patterns seen in males with normal amounts of testosterone.

- The above work suggests that females and males come into the world somewhat programmed, or are at least somewhat predisposed to certain behavioral, cognitive, and perhaps, emotional styles. The world then exacerbates or ameliorates these sex differences, although not always with the same degree of ease.

  For example, the tendency of young males towards more aggressive play (which studies show has a high correlation with testosterone production) can be greatly enhanced by watching cartoons of action heroes, playing with toy weapons, being reinforced for being tough, etc. However, as most mothers and teachers can attest, the obverse often is not as simple.

The tug between nature and nurture was clearly in evidence when a reading teacher at my previous school enrolled her four-year-old son in our preschool. She had been careful, since his birth, to give him a diverse array of toys, including those that would be labeled stereotypically female and stereotypically male. However, being a serious pacifist, she excluded any form of play weapons or violent games or toys. His television watching and book reading had been chosen with the same care and underlying philosophy. On one unforgettable day, his class was having graham crackers for a snack. This carefully raised boy took the opportunity to bite his graham cracker into the shape of a gun and proceeded to "kill" everyone in the class! I couldn't resist: I ran to get his mother to say that she *had* to come and see her son doing something truly remarkable. Her response: "Is he reading?" My response: "No. Even better... hurry!"

Cognitive

Brain imaging (Magnetic Resonance Imaging, commonly known as MRIs) allows us to watch brains while they are alive and working on something. They have also allowed researchers to watch the development of the brain through the stages of childhood, adolescence, and adulthood. As a result, the structural and functional cognitive differences between males and females are becoming clearer:

- In 1995, when gender research was a hot, new topic, the entire March 27 issue of *Newsweek* was devoted to the topic of the cognitive differences between males and females. Color pictures of male and female brains showed varying patterns by sex as males and females tried to solve the same problem. This mapping of the neurological circuitry shows that most females use many areas of the brain simultaneously to solve a problem while males tend to use far fewer areas of the brain for the same problem.

This data helps explain why the medical profession sees more catastrophic results of localized cerebral damage for males than for females. Whereas males have a more narrow neurological usage pattern, and thus less "geographic area" to compensate for damage to a particular region, females have been using more areas of the brain, and thus have "back up systems."

- Showing the growth of interest and research in this field, *Scientific American* went from eight pages in its May 2005 issue to an entire special issue, "His Brain, Her Brain" in May 2010.

- Other cognitive research shows additional sex differences. Keith E. Beery and Norman A. Buktenica, in their work on visual motor development, showed that females develop their fine motor skills at an earlier age than males. When they developed the widely used test, *The Visual Motor Inventory*, Beery and Buktenica provided standard scoring tables by sex and age to reflect the developmental differences they observed.

- The maturity of the prefrontal cortex (PFC) is critical to decision-making. It is not full-grown until at least age thirty, perhaps even later. While it is growing, it is quite plastic and benefits from use. The growth of a typical girl's PFC is about two years in advance of a typical boy's PFC (e.g., a 10-year-old girl's PFC is about the size of a 12-year-old boy's PFC).

- New research has identified part of the brain called the right Temporal Parietal Junction (rTPJ), as having as its focus the sole task of understanding others. This part of the brain is bigger in females.

- The literature focusing on hormonal and cognitive structural differences between heterosexual and homosexual humans is showing some promise of helping to clarify gender differences. For example, an article in *New Scientist* (June 16, 2008) displays

MRIs of hetero- and homosexual brains indicating the differing patterns in the limbic systems. As reported in the article, "The scans reveal that in gay people, key structures of the brain governing emotion, mood, anxiety and aggressiveness resemble those in straight people of the opposite sex."

- A caveat: Although research is documenting the differences between sexes, there is also diversity within each sex. This seems to account, partially, for the differing opinions of practitioners and parents, as well as for some ambiguous and contradictory research findings.

In summary, the research and literature focusing on neurobiological differences between females and males is becoming clearer. There is still much to be done to refine the data and our understanding of these differences. There is also a growing mandate to look at the present data on sex-related differences and begin to translate them into action: the better parenting and teaching of girls and boys.

Psychological Research and Literature

Self-Esteem

Self-esteem is a critical element in a child's performance, behavior, and the ability to make choices; inequity in the treatment of females is a key factor in the loss of self-esteem.

Much has been written on this topic. Therefore, the focus here will be on the recent research that looks at self-esteem in relation to sex and gender differences. This may be a good place to underscore the difference in the terms sex and gender. Here are very simple and general definitions:

- Sex: Your biology, being a girl or a boy. "I am a girl…"
- Gender: A combination of your biology and how you and the world see and shape you (sociology and psychology added) as a female or a male. "Females are…"

- Because sentences that begin "Females are..." or "Males are..." are often completed in ways that are very damaging, Peggy Macintosh, the associate director of the Wellesley Centers for Women, goes so far as to call gender a "description, prescription, and a lie."

While we are looking at clarifying definitions, please note that the terms "self-concept" and "self-esteem" are often used interchangeably in the literature. For reasons that will become clearer in Chapter Two, the preferred usage in this book will be "self-esteem."

- Because it got a lot of attention in the popular press, the A.A.U.W. study, as it has been labeled, became the best-known representative research in the area of self-esteem. In 1991, the American Association of University Women sponsored this study, which included 3,000 schoolchildren between grades four and ten. Responses of the girls and boys were shown in various charts with percentages by gender.

  The data led the researchers to several conclusions, all of which show patterns that are more negative for girls at all ages than for boys. One important pattern was that girls rated their self-esteem significantly lower than boys rated their self-esteem. This gap increased as the age of the children moved towards adolescence.

  The second powerful pattern was that self-esteem had a much more direct effect on behavior for girls than it did for boys. For example, a girl who thinks she is not good in a particular subject — math or science for instance — most likely will not take an elective advanced-placement course in this area. This correlation is not as significant for boys.

- A girl's self-esteem seems to have a more controlling or enhancing effect on her decisions and behaviors than it does for boys

- On a par with the media attention given to the above work is the research of Carol Gilligan, Lyn Brown, et al. This group of researchers from Harvard spent years completing longitudinal studies of girls at the independent Emma Willard School (New York) and Laurel School (Ohio). The findings are complex and extensive, but in the area of self-esteem, the Gilligan work is supportive of the data and findings of the A.A.U.W. research.

Gilligan has become an icon for feminists and is well known for her writings about the pattern of girls' deteriorating self-esteem resulting in a "loss of voice" by the time they reach adolescence. In the book, *Meeting at the Crossroads*, several poignant interviews show the change in the girls over time.

There is the self-confident second grader who literally blows a whistle at the dinner table because she isn't being heard, contrasted with the senior who jeopardizes her life by riding with a drunk driver rather than saying anything. All of the stories of girls in the ten years between the whistle and the ride show a constant progression of increasing self-doubt and subsequent deterioration of self-esteem.

When Gilligan first presented this work at a symposium in Cleveland, an audible gasp went up from the women in the room as they recognized themselves in her stories

- Additional data supporting the findings of lower self-esteem in girls come from more traditional psychological research such as experiments done with younger children around risk-taking.

In one study, children were asked to decide how far from the peg they would stand in a ring toss game. Most boys chose to stand a good distance away, as if compelled by the risk. Girls, meanwhile, chose to stand very close, almost guaranteeing their success. While this study, in and of it self, does not prove that girls have lower self-esteem than boys, the accumulation of studies with this kind of gender differential provides a mountain of circumstantial evidence that is hard to ignore.

- In the last decade, even more research on girls and self-esteem has been done, my own research included (see *Girls Will be Girls: Raising Competent and Courageous Daughters*). Through all of it, the conclusions reached in the A.A.U.W. study and by Gilligan have been upheld.

For all the improvement we have seen in girls' achievements, a 2008 report found a "self-esteem crisis in this country that permeates every aspect of a girl's life including her looks, performance in school, and relationships with friends and family members." Titled *Real Girls, Real Pressure: A National Report on Self-Esteem*, and conducted by Strategy One for the Dove Self-Esteem Fund, key findings were

- 70% of girls did not believe that they were good enough, or did not measure up in some way

- 75% of girls with low self-esteem reported engaging in negative activities (cutting, eating disorders, bullying, smoking, and drinking)

- Transition to teenage years is the key time during which girls lost their trust in adults

- Positive words and actions from parents are central in fostering positive self-esteem in girls.

Keep in mind that most research is done in Westernized cultures, with a fairly high proportion of the participants being white and part of a narrow socioeconomic band. More recent work is being done with African-American and Latino girls, preliminarily indicating some variations. More data are needed before reporting any clear trends.

Values/Morality

The literature supports the existence of differing views and beliefs by gender. Females often use a lens of connectedness while males usually choose a lens of justice for their decision-making.

Like self-esteem, values and morality have been the subject of much thought, research, and voluminous publications. However, until Carol Gilligan's 1982 publication of *In a Different Voice*, a comprehensive description, let alone study, of female moral development had not been done. All of the work of major developmentalists like Jean Piaget and Erik Erikson had focused on male development. Likewise, the moral developmentalists, with Lawrence Kohlberg as the most well known, used only males in their studies and then generalized the findings to all human development.

Gilligan's studies of female development have been criticized (the critics charge her work is too subjective, not having enough standardization and clinical controls) because they are dependent on anecdotal accounts that have been coded by her research affiliates. However, thousands of women and girls who have participated in or read Gilligan's research find that their own sense of morality resonates with these anecdotal accounts. Indeed, in my presentations around the country, when discussing these gender differences in morality, the number of women who silently nod in agreement while I am talking always surprises and impresses me.

Simply put, Gilligan's paradigm indicates that *males and females hold very different sets of values that result in differing moral priorities, and therefore, judgments, actions, and feelings.*

According to Gilligan, there are two types of moral orientations. One is labeled justice or fairness; the other is labeled caring or connectedness. All people possess both orientations, but, justice is more dominant in most males and connectedness more dominant in most females. This is a statistical trend with variations (see the concept of "twenty-percenters" in Chapter Two).

- The justice point of view, more prevalent in males, identifies things as good or bad based on an accepted framework of fairness — promises should be kept, stealing is bad, there are no exceptions to the following of laws, etc.

- The connectedness point of view, held by most females, is

more situational. Thus, breaking a promise so as not to hurt someone's feelings is acceptable, or lying to a teacher to protect a friend is honorable, not a breach of the honor code.

Gilligan and subsequent writers and researchers contend that most laws in society and rules in schools are based on the justice (male) orientation of moral development. This often results in females being penalized or degraded for their moral beliefs or actions — or leaves them feeling out of synch. Some psychologists contend that this is one of the bases for the downward trend in self-esteem as females experience more of the world's consequences and social mores.

My own work indicates that *how* consequences are explained or meted out to girls can help them become weaker or stronger. For example, letting a girl know that a particular transgression is a misstep and that you believe in her and expect that she will learn from this, often has a very positive effect on growth and self-esteem. Whereas, saying, "What is wrong with you!" begins to erode self-esteem.

Please note: it is very important to keep the consequence or punishment while being supportive of the girl. Remember, don't "throw out the baby with the bath water."

The honor codes that exist in many schools are good examples of this difficulty. A typical honor code tenet is that a person who knows of an honor code offense must report it to the appropriate school person or be held as guilty and accountable as the transgressor.

In one girls' school that had such an honor code, an "underground" method of dealing with such situations evolved. When someone saw a peer cheat during a test, instead of reporting the infraction, she would either tell a trusted adult in the school community and ask for advice, or tell the transgressor that she had seen what happened and hoped that the girl would not do it again or would "confess" to the appropriate teacher.

When these underground paths became evident, many discussions were held with the teachers and the students in the school community.

After considering what was happening and reviewing the literature on the moral development of females, the school made several changes in the honor code. In essence, the alternatives listed above were legitimized and made a functional and public part of the code.

Affect

The affective system of the brain (also known as the limbic system) is the seat of human emotions. Although the cause is still hotly debated, the literature indicates that females are somewhat more predisposed to certain emotions and emotional patterns than males are in the same situation or given circumstances.

A caveat: Next to the nature/nurture debate, this topic causes the most heated discussions and arguments. It also has the greatest potential to be over generalized and become sexist in its interpretation. Therefore, great care needs to be exercised in extrapolating the data to implications and practice. The only area of agreement is that we don't know as much as we would like, and a great deal of additional study is necessary.

Having said this, many educators and psychologists do believe that the affective domain has significant impact on beliefs and behaviors:

- Experienced coaches, educators, business executives and the like know that capturing the affective system of individuals or groups can make the difference between success and failure. Leaders throughout history have recognized intuitively the power of the limbic system (the seat of emotions in the brain) over the cortex (the home of rational thought).

- Whether it is a result of nature, nurture, or both, women, in general, express, and seem to be influenced by their feelings differently than men are influenced by their feelings. Mary Belenky, et al, devoted a whole book on the topic: *Women's Ways of Knowing*.

- Most teachers have had the experience of having a girl feel that the teacher does not like her because of the grades she has been given by that teacher. A male physics teacher found that when boys came to him for extra help, they typically just wanted to get down to work and solve the problem. Girls, however, wanted to discuss how they were feeling about their difficulties and to be reassured by the teacher.

- The 1991 A.A.U.W. study has examples of girls avoiding courses based on affective factors related to grades, while in similar circumstances, many boys attribute the poor grades or failure to a teacher and continue to perform and take courses in that particular subject area or with that particular teacher. My ongoing observations and research show these same patterns are as prevalent now as they were when the study was first made.

- One of the best early sources of current research on sex differences in learning is the book *Mathematics and Gender* by Elizabeth Fennema and Gilah Leder. Many of the studies are not related just to the subject of math. Under the topic, "Internal Beliefs," the authors conclude that "affective variables have a more important influence on the achievement and participation of females than they do for males."

- Mary Belenky takes these data and suggests that teachers who take the affective component seriously and structure their classrooms, styles of teaching, and curriculum around this knowledge are much more successful with girls than teachers who do not take these factors into account. She dubs these teachers "connected teachers." The literature surrounding cooperative learning also supports this point of view.

- More recently there has been a lot of research on emotional differences in male and female brains. One only has to "google" the key words to see a very large list. For example, Larry Cahill, et. al., found sex differences in emotional memory.

- These findings show that females tend to use more of the left amygdala for emotional memory storage, while males use more of the right amydala. Since the left amygdala focuses more on details of emotion and the right amygdala more on overview emotions, you can begin to see why sex stereotypes develop.

  For example: my mother remembered that the smell of gardenias at her wedding made her smile, and my father remembered that there was a wedding and there were flowers there, probably...

Much more data and resources can be found in such books as *The Female Brain* by Louann Brizendine, and other references at the end of this book.

Educational Research and Literature

School Structure

The research points to structural components of a school or system that can and do influence gender equity. Those reported as positive for girls include single-gender settings that are democratic and collaborative.

One of the clearest areas of research in the last several years is the area of single-gender learning environments. Whether it is single-gender schools, single-gender classes within coeducational schools, or single-gender groupings of students within coeducational classes, the research supports these structures as having some advantages for females.

Girls in these situations generally get better grades, report that they learn more and are more positive about the learning situation, have higher self-esteem, and more often move on to advanced courses than do girls in regular coeducational situations.

In 1992, the U.S. Department of Education published a summary of the previous twenty years of research on single-gender versus co-educational schools. The general conclusion was that all of the studies supported single-gender schools as better learning environments for girls. Since that time, similar data have been accumulating.

In acknowledgment of the importance of such research, the South Carolina Department of Education recently asked *all* public school districts to begin to offer some type of single-sex educational options for their students. This movement has the support of the state superintendent who created a state-level position to coordinate the single-gender initiative. In an article in *Advances in Gender and Education*, David Chadwell emphasizes some of the keys to success:

- Choice (make it an opportunity, not a requirement)

- Make gender a school-wide focus, not limited to the single-sex classes

- Support the teachers, especially with professional development

- Focus on procedures, not lessons

- Communicate, communicate, communicate

Another article in the same 2009 issue of *Gender and Education* talks about a public school (the Dr. Walter Cunningham School for Excellence in Waterloo, Iowa) that has had a single-sex boys' and single-sex girls' second grade class since 2003. The article underscores the importance of understanding gender differences, stressing that to be "successful gender-specific teachers means that we have to first recognize the fundamental differences between sexes and then develop instructional strategies based on those biological differences in our classroom curriculum." The success of this approach was encapsulated in these words: "The girls were doing more than just excelling in math and science; they were reaching for the stars and never looking back."

Two good sources of data are the websites for the National Coalition of Girls Schools (NCGS) and the National Association for Single Sex Public Education (NASSPE). Look especially for the NASSPE's peer-reviewed journal, *Advances in Gender and Education*. All of these resources and more are given at the end of this book.

Classroom Structures

Research dramatically supports single-gender classes, especially in middle and high schools.

The data on single-gender classes in coeducational schools are just as dramatic as the data for single-gender schools. Most of the classes have been at the middle school or high school level and in the areas of math or science. Also, most attempts at creating single-gender classes in coeducational schools have occurred in the independent school world, although in the last few years this has become a popular trend in many public school districts (e.g., The Leadership Schools in New York City, Dallas, Dayton, and elsewhere). NASSPE maintains a detailed list that is updated monthly.

In the original Title IX legislation in 1975, single-sex classes were allowed only on an extremely limited basis (charter schools, sex education classes, and gym classes involving contact sports). The American Civil Liberties Union (ACLU) found this discriminatory and brought suit against school districts who were offering single-gender opportunities.

These suits had a chilling effect until 2006 when the Bush administration relaxed the rules and permitted school districts to create single-sex schools and classes as long as enrollment was voluntary and "substantially equal" opportunities (in number and quality) were offered for the excluded sex, or on a coeducational basis. This change has had a pervasive and positive effect on public school efforts and many single-gender offerings began as soon as the new rules went into effect.

Despite the concerns of the ACLU and others, when care is taken in creating single-sex programs, and teachers are sufficiently trained, the reports about all-girls classes in both public and private schools, indicate that these classes are successful. School personnel report significant positive results for girls participating in single-gender classes:

- "It was one of the most positive changes we have ever made," said Joan Lutton, head of the Cushman School (Florida). "The girls' self-images rose immediately."

- When asked for words of wisdom for schools contemplating the creation of single-gender classes, Nancy Calhoun, middle school head at The Walker School (Georgia), said, "Do it!" She went on to say that "girls, at first, overwhelmed the teachers with questions. They were so enthusiastic they voluntarily asked for and attended after-school sessions. Their achievement was truly impressive."

- Pam Belitski, seventh-grade math teacher at the Anacapa Middle School (California), added, "The classroom atmosphere is more productive...girls are aggressively exploring with manipulatives, measuring, and problem solving, and becoming divergent thinkers. This school year the girls' math class has increased three times from its original size."

- Catherine C. Veal, director of communications, Illinois Mathematics and Science Academy (Illinois) said "Students in the all-female class displayed greater performance-level growth on quizzes, homework, and class exams than did females in the coeducational section taught by the same teacher...More females...enrolled in and successfully completed Calculus-Based Physics than ever before. There was a strikingly different quality to the atmosphere, character, and climate of the all-female class. The learning community that emerged was characterized by a profound sense of responsibility for learning, a special rapport between and among the teacher and the students, a spirit of co-learning, with both the teacher and the students feeling free to ask questions, admit mistakes, take risks, express confusion, etc."

Linda J. Sax, an Associate Professor of Education at UCLA published an illuminating study in 2008 titled, *Women Graduates of Single-Sex and Coeducational High Schools: Differences in their Characteristics and the Transition to College.* Her study is of particular interest because it draws on large, national sample of 6,552 female graduates of 225 private single-sex high schools and 14,684 female graduates of 1,169 private coeducational high schools. While calling for more research, Professor Sax reports that most of the results she found were "favorable to single-sex graduates" including the following "statistically significant differences" for female graduates of single-sex schools:

- Showed *greater academic engagement* as measured by time spent on homework and on studying (on their own and with other students), tutoring other students, and talking with teachers outside of class.

- Had *higher SAT scores.* Mean SAT composite scores were 43 points higher for single-sex graduates.

- Expressed a *greater interest in attending graduate school* and often chose a college based on its ability to get its graduates into top graduate schools.

- Had *higher academic self-confidence* as expressed in more of them rating themselves as "above average" or in the "highest 10 percent" for academic ability, intellectual self-confidence, writing ability, and speaking ability.

- Had *higher confidence in their mathematical ability and computer skills.*

- Expressed a *greater interest in a career in Engineering.*

- Indicated a *stronger predisposition to participation in co-curricular activities.*

- Exhibited *greater political engagement* through frequency of political discussion with friends and in class, and, by reporting that it was "very important" or "essential" for them to keep up to date on political affairs.

While the report emphasizes the benefits of a single-sex setting for girls, especially in those areas like math and science that have traditionally favored boys, it ends with a strong call for further research, raising the following questions:

- How and why do single-sex schools produce positive outcomes and which conditions can be transferred to coeducational schools?

- Which types of students benefit most from single-sex education?

- Do the benefits of single-sex education persist throughout college and beyond?

- How do the benefits of single-sex education compare for males versus females?

I would add to their list an area in which some research is already showing that there are positive outcomes: what are the benefits for African-American boys/girls in a single-sex setting?

Other structural (e.g., traditional classroom vs round tables) and environmental areas are shown in the literature on single-gender schools or single-gender classes to be beneficial for girls. That is, girls perform better and report more satisfaction and confidence in democratic, cooperative, connected, inclusive, hands-on educational settings.

Professional groups from the National Council for Teachers of Math (in their publication on math standards) to the National Association for the Education of Young Children (in their developmentally appropriate practices for young children) to the Association for School Curriculum Development (in their annual report on curriculum research) all support the above structures for girls, as well as boys, in most situations.

A few qualifiers are in order. Competition seems to work well for boys and a minority of girls and should not be deleted totally from the educational world. Likewise, authoritarian, directed teaching is useful and effective in instances of advanced placement courses, preparation for information-based exams, etc. In addition, teaching splinter skills absent from meaningful integration or understanding is useful for students who have a particular disability or low aptitude in a particular area.

In other words, all educational structures and pedagogical techniques have their place. The difficult part is knowing when to impose which structure and when to use a particular technique based on the group or individual needs of the learners. This is why teachers should earn more money than pitchers on professional baseball teams! The needs of individual learners or differing learning styles compel us to maintain a huge array of pedagogical tools in our educational toolboxes.

Curriculum

What textbooks are used, what is taught, and the equity and inclusiveness of the curriculum, all influence learners.

Peggy Macintosh, the Associate Director of the Wellesley Centers for Women, has been the recognized guru in this area for many years. Please consult her and say that I sent you!

Seriously, much work has been done at the Wellesley Center, as well as at many other colleges and universities. It is not very profound to say that females feel disconnected when courses are all about wars and male achievements, or that male-oriented language (e.g., the generic "mankind" for "humankind" or alumni to mean both male and female graduates in a co-ed school) has a deleterious effect on readers, or that learning is more meaningful when it is related to something meaningful in the learner's world. This observation is not very profound, but these practices are also not very well adhered to in the educational world. It is one area that can be analyzed clearly by looking at texts and materials to make them inclusive, fair, and meaningful.

Pedagogy

How each teacher influences the learning and interaction in the classroom. Some techniques are gender fair, others are not. Those techniques that the research supports as positive for girls are not negative for boys.

Much of this has been implied in the above sections. In terms of relevance to gender, there are at least five areas of clear focus in the literature:

- Airtime
- Modeling/Mentoring
- Hands-on experiences
- Cooperative learning
- Connectedness.

Before we go any further, I want to point out the key difficulty with pedagogical research. Two questions immediately come to mind when confronting the results of a study. First, why is this so? And, second, why does it matter? Unfortunately, research rarely answers why questions. Almost any research is correlational (showing the relationship between things), not causal. To prove causation requires a rigorous and rigid research design with control groups. One group receives one "treatment," e.g. spelling workbooks; one group receives another "treatment," e.g., whole language literature books, and one group receives no "treatment," that is, does not focus on spelling at all. You can see that this paradigm would not be acceptable under most circumstances in the educational world, because the "no treatment" control group needs to be there to prove that improvement in spelling is not the result of natural growth and development. Few schools, teachers, parents, or students would allow a control group to receive no treatment regardless of how important it could be in making conclusions about pedagogy and learning.

Air Time — The first area of pedagogy to consider is "air time," a term that was derived from the work of researchers who focused, literally, on the air waves of the classroom by observing, videotaping, categorizing, and tallying the interactions in classrooms of various grade levels in various types of schools. This area of research had been quite consistent since the first edition was published of the iconic

1994 book, *Failing at Fairness* by Myra and David Sadker. They reported that compared to boys, girls are:

- Five times less likely to receive the most attention from teachers
- Three times less likely to be praised
- Eight times less likely to call out in class
- Half as likely to demand help or attention
- Half as likely to be called on in class

There has been quite a reversal in some of the above listed areas. Equity seems to still be very illusive in most classrooms, but there has been a significant shift since the Sadker's work. In my own research, teachers report that boys are "higher maintenance" in terms of movement, noise and behavioral issues. Therefore, they often demand more teacher time and attention in these areas. However, when it comes to asking questions, answering questions, and seeking help, girls dominate the "air time."

It turns out that the earlier research was accurate, but not sufficiently nuanced in its understanding. Check out the excellent article, *Differential Teacher Attention to Boys and Girls* by Beaman et al. in the August 2006 issue of *Education Review*. The authors do a fair, and complex job of reviewing and synthesizing the research in this area, and its progression over time, first showing the disadvantage to boys, then to girls, then a subtle understanding of how each group can be advantaged/disadvantaged depending on the teacher's understanding of classroom dynamics. A few of their findings:

- The emphasis has shifted away from the number and/or duration of teacher-student interactions to the type of interaction.
- Boys dominate in the classroom because they receive much more negative attention than girls (a good thing or not?). In other words, "teachers do not respond to student sex *per se*, but do respond to their behavior." Hence the idea that "re-

engineering the teaching context with particular emphasis on teacher interactional style, may yield more effective learning environments for girls and boys."

- Although the pendulum on "underachievement by gender" swung from girls to boys, the fact is that "both boys and girls performance levels have been consistently rising"

- More and more teachers describe the ideal student as female. However, one researcher, Debra Myhill, in a 2002 issue of the *British Educational Research Journal*, pointed out that the very qualities that benefit girls in the school environment will be a detriment in the work world: "Few company executives, politicians, lawyers, and so on would be described as compliant and conformist, though their PAs may well be!'

- If girls are the ideal students, then boys are seen, if not disruptive, than as the class clowns. Becky Francis identifies these differences as "boys with 'attitude' (questioning, challenging and 'having a laugh'), and girls as being identified with 'academic application' (characterized by diligence and pleasure in learning)." She goes on to say that "… there is no reason why 'attitude' and academic application should be seen as incompatible.… We should endeavour [sic] to encourage both 'attitude' and application in all our pupils, irrespective of their gender, and this may be the key to improving achievement. Yet, in order to do so we will need to deconstruct the oppositional construction that locates attitude in the male, and application in the female, in the classroom."

- Finally, much is being written about gender and learning disabilities with the emphasis on the over diagnosis of boys by "pathologizing" normal boyish behavior. However, research supports an unfortunate sort of equity here, for just as boys are being over-diagnosed, girls, because of their "under the radar" good behavior, are being under-diagnosed.

Catherine Krupnick, (who produced a seminal report, *Women and Men in the Classroom: Inequality and Its Remedies*, while at Harvard University), suggests, along with many other teacher trainers, a variety of methods for reducing the imbalance of airtime in schools. Foremost among these are the following techniques that I recommend in educational workshops:

- Waiting a few seconds before allowing anyone to answer a question

- Having students write down key words for their response before they respond orally to a discussion/question

- Repeating the previous person's response before giving a response

- Equity techniques such as giving each student three chips to "spend" during a class — everyone has to talk three times — no more, no less

- Putting students into small groups

- Arranging the seating so that all the talkers are not clustered together

- Structuring tasks so that everyone has a task, question, or topic to share with the rest of the class

- Encouraging the students to keep response tallies for a period of time to help with decisions about "air" equity in the classroom

- Literally taking turns — a boy's response, then a girl's response, and so on

- Establishing rules of discourse, such as "you may not put down anyone's answers"

This list could continue, but the gist is clear. If there are not constraints, structures, or guidelines in coeducational classrooms of all ages, the research shows that an imbalance of airtime occurs in most classrooms.

In my observations of hundreds of classrooms, unless a teacher employs one or more of the above techniques, the interactions between the teacher and the students are inequitable. But in which sex's favor? IT DEPENDS! It depends on the age of students, control methods of teachers, subject area, ratio of boys to girls, etc. For example, a teacher who has a very low tolerance for movement or noise in her/his classroom may spend a great deal of time talking to and dealing with active boys. A teacher who likes to only call on volunteers will give more time to whoever volunteers the most (and that changes dramatically by subject area, type of questions, etc.).

Regardless of the causation, experience shows that the imbalance can be countermanded by a variety of not-so-difficult-to-employ techniques and the increased awareness of the key players: teachers and students. However, a warning is needed here — in classrooms where teachers have altered their behavior in the direction of parity, it is very difficult to get some of the students who are not accustomed to participating to participate. The thorny problem of how to get girls with low self-esteem to talk will be covered in a later chapter.

Modeling/Mentoring — A second area of pedagogy is the use of modeling and mentoring. Studies in this area have demonstrated that while a brief contact with a model/mentor (such as a career day) can have some impact, the best results come when the connection is sustained over time. In this case, the presence of a mentor can lead to dramatic improvement in the self-esteem and performance of girls.

The book, *What Kids Need to Succeed: Proven, Practical Ways to Raise Good Kids*, discusses the results of a survey of more than 270,000 young people in 600 communities across the country. The authors identified thirty assets that every youngster needs. Number four on the list: "having adults, besides parents, who can provide advice and support." Some examples of successful mentor programs:

- According to a 2007 Public/Private Ventures study of Big

Brothers Big Sisters of America's school-based mentoring programs serving youth in grades four through nine, kids who have mentors improve in a range of behaviors. They have an overall improvement in academic performance, especially in science, and written and oral language. The quality of their class work improves along with number of assignments completed, both in and out of class. Serious school infractions, like fighting, decrease, and attendance increases. More important, kids with mentors report a feeling of increased academic competency.

• Next to single-gender classes, programs in schools that include mentors and modeling have the most positive impact on the achievement and attitude of girls. "Take Your Daughter to Work Day" is a very public example of this. From the very first "day" over sixteen years ago positive reports from girls across the nation appeared in newspapers and were heard in classrooms by teachers. Now expanded to "Take Our Sons and Daughters to Work Day," their website is a good source for resources and activities.

• Prompted by the very high drop-out rate of female science or math majors, universities are experimenting with all-female math and science dorms. The Bunting-Cobb dormitory at Rutgers University houses 100 female undergraduate students in science, mathematics and engineering. Female graduate students act as mentors and models for each other and for undergraduate women. And, professors often stop in and have discussions with the residents. So this becomes, in essence, a live-in mentoring/modeling experience.

Females who live in this dorm have extinguished the significant difference in gender drop out rates in these traditionally male dominated areas.

• Across Ages, offered by the Community Action Commission

(CAC) pairs adult mentors 45 and older with adolescents aged 10-14 years old. "The mentors serve as role models who help the children and teens improve their grades, make better lifestyle decisions, and learn to cope with peer pressure."

- *Parade* magazine, in its April 25, 2010 issue, highlighted Girls in the Game, which serves 2500 Chicago area girls age 6 to 17. GIG runs after-school programs in 30 schools and parks, holds game days, and has a summer camp. Adult coaches are assisted by teen leaders who can earn scholarship money for college; and the first group of teen leaders has all gone on to college.

- Many middle schools are experimenting with mentoring programs for girls at this critical and fragile developmental stage of life. The Urban Community School in Cleveland, for example, was worried about the dropout and pregnancy rate of girls from their middle school. They instituted a program that paired each girl with a working adult female. If a girl had a dream about being a veterinarian, her partner was a female veterinarian. Mentors and "mentees" met at school once a month for lunch and the girls made several visits each year to their mentors' places of work.

  The results were as expected: dropout and pregnancy rates plummeted, grades improved, girls reported higher levels of self-esteem. UCS was the first elementary school in Cleveland to receive the Excellence in Education Award from the U.S. Department of Education and was recently named a School of Excellence by the Cleveland Foundation and the George Gund Foundations.

- The middle school age group is also a target area for most STEM (Science, Technology, Engineering and Math) programs. As reported in the AAUW's 2004 report *Under the Microscope: A Decade of Gender Equity Projects in the Sciences*, "Studies have revealed that gender differences in attitudes and interest in science are present by the end of the elementary grades," but it is "During middle school, the gap in boys' and girls' interest in science appears to grow."

For example, the Massachusetts's Institute of Technology (MIT) runs a five-week summer STEM program, taught by MIT undergraduates, and follows up with a nine-month school year program that pairs MIT student mentors by interest with their middle school mentees.

- Another similar program run by the Worcester Polytechnic Institute (WPI) of Massachusetts is a two-week summer residential program for 30 girls entering seventh grade. The program is based on best practices for engineering outreach programs and offers a variety of follow-up and mentoring activities during the school year. The program has reported a variety of positive outcomes but the proof in the pudding is that Camp Reach attendees were "significantly more likely to attend a public high school specializing in mathematics and science and also more likely to enroll in computer science and other elective STEM courses in high school (not including Calculus and Physics)."

- Washington State Institute for Public Policy studies of the mentoring program in the state's juvenile justice system has an important reminder for us. The 2002 report looked at participants records 12 months after they completed a mentoring program and found that mentoring reduced recidivism, or re-offending, and returned $3.58 of benefit to society for every dollar spent. However, it is significant that a 2006 follow-up study found that all benefits had disappeared, reminding us of the importance of putting in place long-term programs, rather than looking for a magic silver bullet.

Hands-on Experiences: Doing — The third area of pedagogy to consider is "doing." Don't just talk about it, read about it, or think about it — *do* it. Whatever the "it" is, research supports the act of experiencing/doing as key to long-term effects on the doer. Even the current brain research is supporting doing. The brain is quite plastic, and as an area becomes robust (ready for use) it is important to use it to make it strong and effective. There is a saying in the brain field: "use it or lose it." It means that the brain is designed to get better, stronger and bigger, just like a muscle, when the parts are used early and frequently. That's what promotes healthy development. Different parts of the brain are impacted by doing something instead of just thinking about it.

This area is hard to label, but easy to understand. Projects, labs, building, manipulatives, games, hands-on activities, volunteering are all good options. But the word "doing" is so nice and clean and simple! There is an old Chinese proverb that says:

I hear and forget.

I see and remember.

I do and I understand.

Whatever you call it, research, experience, logic, and common sense all tell us that "doing" is a very effective way of embedding something in our long-term memory banks thereby increasing the likelihood of it having a longer-term impact on the person.

All of the many current books on effective teaching/learning for females promote hands-on learning as very beneficial for girls. One clear school example is the math curriculum *Everyday Mathematics,* a math program for grades PK-6 supported by the Center for Elementary Mathematics and Science Education at the University of Chicago. This is the program that I recommend most to schools, especially girls' schools. The program does what its title implies: it relates arithmetic and mathematical thinking to everyday life situations and is filled with hands-on experiential learning. The results for girls who stay with this program for several years are quite impressive.

Cooperative Learning — This is a huge umbrella term. In general, cooperative learning refers to not working as an individual, but with one or more others. Later in this book, there will be data and information supporting the conclusion that, because of neurobiological predispositions, girls' learning can be enhanced by cooperative learning in many situations.

Simply put, girls report that working with others often reduces their fear and anxiety, makes them feel more comfortable and willing to take risks and attempt challenging tasks, increases their interest in a task, prolongs attention and often leads to higher levels of learning. There is a definite place for a considerable amount of cooperative learning in the education of girls.

Keep in mind, though, that girls do need to be able to take risks, learn, and persevere on their own. Individual work will continue to be an important component of helping a girl to become as competent and courageous as she can be.

Connectedness — I'm not sure where to put connectedness in this book. However, it is of such importance, that it will appear in several chapters. The word refers to the need, and want, to be a meaningful part of something: a group, a family, something larger than self. In terms of pedagogy, it certainly is a very big part of the justification for cooperative learning, but it is also more than that.

There is a large body of work referred to as "connected teaching" literature. In my workshops for teachers I have boiled it down to this — the data (letter grades, etc.), as well as what girls themselves report, supports that girls learn better if

- They believe a teacher cares about them.
- They believe the teacher cares about teaching and the subject matter.

In other words, if a teacher feels connected to them and his/her teaching or subject area, that connectedness has a significant positive effect on the learning of girls. I can't begin to count the number of girls that I've interviewed who have underscored these two factors in some way while talking about what helps them learn or about the characteristics of a good teacher.

In Summary

Airtime techniques, modeling and mentors; and, hands-on learning, cooperative learning and connectedness are important and
oft-repeated themes in all of the gender pedagogical research. Please
check out the resources at the end of this book. It contains the most
recent and comprehensive strategies, techniques, and methods for
effective teaching/learning of girls. If you consult these, you will find
a wealth of ideas and be considered for the Who's Who of Well-Read
Professionals in the Field of Gender and Education.

Backlash Literature

When the AAUW conducted its first research in 1885, it reported
the earthshaking results that higher education was *not* injurious to a
women's health! More than a hundred years later, the AAUW published another report that challenged currently held notions about
girls and education. Other research and reports followed as the field
of "gender equity" came into its own. Heavy media coverage brought
it to public attention and fast on its heels came authors who dis-
agreed, often with outrage. The core of their argument was that the
world had changed and inequities no longer existed.

After more than a decade of research focusing on females (what I
call the A.G. decade: After Gilligan), their needs and the inequities
that affect them, several articles appeared that could be called the
"You've Come a Long Way, Baby" literature. The position, simply
stated, was that there is no need to talk about unlevel playing fields
or how schools cheat girls, since things have changed so much for
females recently. The 1980s: girls are shortchanged; the 1990s backlash
literature: no they are not; there is equity.

Two leaders of the backlash literature were Diane Ravitch, previous
director of the Department of Education under the first Bush administration, and Christina Hoff-Summers, a published psychologist.

One of the best and most condensed discussions of this topic
appeared in a *New York Times* (February 13, 1994) article written

by Catherine S. Manegold. She quotes Diane Ravitch's own words: "How can you be a victim when you have succeeded?" Ms. Ravitch asked this question while pulling up a computer file showing female gains in such traditionally male studies as algebra, geometry, and chemistry. "When do we declare victory? When we are at 60 percent of the college population? When we are at 70 percent?"

Well, welcome to the next decade: the 2000s. Symbolizing the change: Barbie! Yes, Barbie. In 1992 Mattel produced a controversial version of a Barbie that was programmed to say, "Math class is tough." Now, the same company has just announced Computer Engineer Barbie. Her accessories were decided on in consultation with the Society of Women Engineers and the National Academy of Engineering. She has a Smartphone and Bluetooth headset. But not everything has changed, her glasses and her laptop are still her trademark hot pink!

An even more notable change: most of the popular press now focuses on the inequity for boys. Was Diane Ravitch a visionary? Medical schools are reporting a gender imbalance in favor of females for the first time in their history. The New York Times recently reported on the social problems that ensue at colleges where women outnumber men. Girls' scores on SATs and ACTs are significantly higher than boys. I could go on…. The 2000s: the decade of the shortchanged boys.

As always, the truth is a little more nuanced than that. The AAUW's 2008 report, *Where the Girls Are: The Facts About Gender Equity in Education*, took "a comprehensive look at girls' educational achievement during the past 35 years, paying special attention to the relationship between girls' and boys' progress." This study uncovered three key facts about gender equity in schools today:

- Girls' successes don't come at boys' expense. That is, "in states where girls do well on tests, boys also do well, and states with low test scores among boys tend to also have low scores among girls."

- On average, girls' and boys' educational performance has improved.

- Understanding disparities by race/ethnicity and family income level is critical to understanding girls' and boys' achievement.

Oh, and about that article in the NYT; it turns out that although "women are attending and graduating from high school and college at a higher rate than are their male peers" men are still not the losers as "the proportion of young men graduating from high school and earning college degrees today is at an all-time high."

If girls' success also means boys' success, then where does the problem lie? The AAUW report concludes that, "the crisis is not specific to boys; rather, it is a crisis for African American, Hispanic, and low-income children."

This new edition of *How Girls Thrive* is being published at the start of the second decade of the twenty-first century. Let me rush to grab onto the pendulum and muscle it into the center: we need to do a better job of raising and teaching all children, keeping in mind that girls and boys *are somewhat different and often need somewhat different strategies and approaches.*

Let me be one of the first to name this decade: The Equity (not equality) Decade.

Conclusion

This chapter is not meant to be an exhaustive look at the literature but an overview to help the adults in the lives of girls become more knowledgeable about sex and gender issues. I hope that this knowledge base will help in the task of analyzing a system (e.g., school, division, department, class, family or community) and then making decisions about what can be done to create a learning and living environment for all children that is equitable and effective.

CHAPTER 2

External and Internal Constraints

"A good idea will keep you awake during the morning, but a great idea will keep you awake during the night." — Marilyn Van Savant

First, A Note to Parents

At first — and even second glance — this chapter may seem to be just for educators. But don't let all the talk of teaching and the examples using schools fool you; there is a great deal in this chapter of importance for parents. It just takes a little imagination to see how families are like mini-organizations, and how the concepts of internal and external constraints can be applied to any individual in a family. This chapter will also help parents and educators to better communicate about the needs of the student/daughter while keeping in mind the understandable constraints of a given school's structure and personnel. So, if you are not an educator, don't skip this chapter, you may miss some of the key pearls for your strand.

Why Constraints Matter

The first chapter made it clear that gender imbalances in schools and organizations (families too) exist and need to be addressed. Yet the process of identifying the areas of gender imbalance, determining the factors involved, and deciding upon strategies for action is very complex. This may explain why even very good schools and institutions hesitate to tackle the problem of gender equity in any systematic way.

Typically, schools have looked at visible external factors that could, or do, influence gender equity, such as structure of classes or pedagogical techniques. When external changes are made that yield positive results, the process of change is often considered successful and complete.

The most common example is a school that provides gender workshops for their teachers. The teachers then go forth and use equity techniques such as wait time in a discussion class or more cooperative and team learning. Although the beneficial effects are apparent, they are not enough. There are still individuals who do not participate in the discussion or the newly formed cooperative group because of internal constraints — low self-esteem being paramount among these.

It is important, therefore, for all schools to carefully examine both the external and internal factors that lead to gender inequity in their communities.

External Constraints

Because external constraints are so much easier to identify, schools concerned about gender equity often begin with collection of numerical data. Usually the data reveal concerns like these that are provided by the Association of School and College Leaders (ASCL) in their 2008 report:

- 32% of secondary school heads were women (down from 40% the previous year).

- 75% of primary school heads were women (lower than the percentage of primary teachers).

In my work in independent, parochial and public schools in the last decade, gender equity in any area is rare. The stereotypic imbalances are alive and well in most schools and in most areas. For example, in teaching positions

- Science and math departments have more male teachers and leaders

- The IT department is often totally male

- Early childhood is almost exclusively populated by female teachers and leaders

The same types of numerical gender imbalances often occur in the ratios of female to male students in particular subject areas, like math and science (a gap that widens by grade level), or with special needs (I've *never* been in a coed school with fewer than a significant majority of boys in the remedial reading programs), as well as elected and appointed leadership positions.

A judgment is being made that numerical imbalances can cause inequities in the educational opportunities for and/or the treatment of either gender. Research in this area is increasingly ferreting out the underlying causes for this hypothesis. Meanwhile, experienced educators and the anecdotal reports of students tend to substantiate this claim. For instance, girls and their teachers report that girls talk in class far less when there are many more boys than girls. This is an example of the data from the "airtime" studies referred to earlier.

Keeping in mind the knowledge about gender and what is beneficial for girls (and boys) as a guiding philosophy, schools might try these strategies for the above inequities:

- When openings occur, find and hire highly qualified females for administrative positions in the school.

- Create a better gender balance of teachers in subject areas and divisions of a school.

- Bring in outside female speakers for science classes; form an affiliation with a graduate school and provide internships for female science students.

- Have co-leaders (one boy, one girl) chosen or elected for student leadership positions.

- Have guidance personnel encourage nontraditional courses for each gender.

Data collection and analysis help to identify external factors that contribute to inequity. Each school needs to be flexible and creative in identifying which imbalances are worth correcting based on the data, the school's philosophy and mission, the board's priorities, cost factors, etc. It is conceivable, for instance, that a school would choose not to alter the varsity imbalance if eighty percent of the school body were female. On the other hand, the school may want to identify admission strategies for attracting more male students to the school!

Some numerical imbalances are not controversial and some simple strategies can make immediate and highly visible positive equity changes. However, others are more complicated or controversial, and you then need to identify whether the imbalances are due to external factors, internal factors, or a combination of the two. It may be that strategies can be used which have multiplicative positive effects. Keep reading if this sounds fuzzy; the clouds will part soon.

External Constraints and Possible Remedies

Let's look at some of the reasons for imbalances. As noted, external constraints or barriers are often easier to identify. This is somewhat confusing as a term, but, put simply, external constraints are external to the person being constrained. Therefore, a chauvinist teacher's beliefs can be an external constraint to the females in his class (even though his belief system is internal to him!).

Here are some examples of external constraints, and possible remedies:

Constraint: The gymnasium is fully utilized and there are no more periods available to increase the P.E. offerings for girls. The external constraints may be limited space and/or scheduling difficulties.

Remedies:

- Offer a P.E. class in another area of the school, e.g., dance in the dance studio.

- Use community spaces such as the community swimming pool.

- Convince donors of the inequity and build another gym.

Constraint: Although sharing the math faculty between the middle and upper school could gender balance a male-dominated math department in the upper school, the schedules are different for each division and do not allow crossover teaching. The external constraint is the different schedules.
Remedies:

- Change to an all-school schedule that will allow crossover teaching.

- Retrain teachers and have some upper-school teachers become middle school teachers.

- Take advantage of openings to hire more female math teachers in the upper school

Constraint: The teacher uses equal participation discussion techniques, but since there is a 5 to 1 ratio of boys to girls in this class, the girls' participation has not increased. The external constraint is the number of boys and the number of girls. (There may also be internal constraints operating — more about this later.)
Remedies:

- Create gender-balanced sub-groups for girls.

- Combine with other sections of the class and redistribute according to gender numerical equity.

- Consider if there are ways to attract more girls to the class in the future by changing the course description, or rescheduling it so it doesn't conflict with more "girl friendly" offerings.

As you can see by the suggestions offered for each situation, options for removing or reducing external constraints can differ markedly in difficulty, cost, resistance, and philosophy. There is no easy-to-follow formula that says, "If you find this, then do this."

Each school needs to identify the gender issues and respond with actions that fit its system, or choose not to act and provide data and justification for that decision.

This is a good time to offer a caveat. External constraints are usually in place for one or more reasons. Even though it may make sense, or it is the "right" thing to do to remove them, there will be resistance to change.

Resistance

Resistance *always* happens when change is proposed or begun. There are no exceptions to this one: not one, not ever. The reason is simple. If there were no forces or beliefs in contradiction to the proposals or change, the change would have happened already. Either people tend to believe in what they are doing or they have become comfortable and change is not received with open arms. If everyone agreed with every change, there would be no consistency and sanity in the world. So, now you see that resistance to change is not only normal, but it is also a positive characteristic of a healthy institution.

Remember, then, through any attempt to bring about change, look for resistance and include plans for overcoming resistance in everything that you do. Do this in advance of any proposed change! Often it can be helpful to engage a consultant to help identify resistance and to create a plan for responding. A consultant can be perceived as more objective and can also say some things very directly and then leave town!

Or, if you can't afford to hire the consultant, and you only have time to read just one book about change, make it *Managing Transitions, 2nd Edition* by William Bridges.

Internal Constraints

Schools often find that after (fill in the blank) years of "successful coeducation" there are still some problems. The reason often is that although they have done a god job of anticipating and ameliorating the external constraints, they have missed or ignored the more difficult internal ones.

Given the previous definition of external constraint, it follows that the term internal constraint refers to the internal state of the person(s) being constrained. The gender research identifies self-esteem as the most powerful of the internal constraints. Additional constraints could be such things as ability or talent, training or knowledge, mental or emotional health.

The logical action would be to remove or reduce the internal constraints. We have just arrived at the wall! Unfortunately, logic alone cannot help generate effective actions for internal restraints. This is true for several reasons.

- First, identification of the cause of the imbalance is very complicated.

- Second, internal constraints can be very resistant to change. If, for example, a girl does not go on to calculus because she experiences severe math anxiety, strategies for overcoming math anxiety often take a long-term commitment, can require professional help, and have no guarantee of success.

- Finally, there is very little agreement in the professional world about how to mold belief systems so that what girls have traditionally done is perceived as positive and appropriate for boys, or vice versa.

Yes, dealing with internal constraints is difficult, but not impossible. They are often the most pervasive constraints in a system and therefore critical to try to tackle and not just weather.

Internal Constraints and Possible Remedies

Constraint — After the algebra II level, it is typical for only 20% of girls to take additional math while 80% of boys do. The internal constraint may be that girls believe they are not capable in math and cannot compete with boys.

Remedy — Beginning with algebra I, create an all-girls section and employ recommended methods for teaching math to girls. Why algebra I? Many girls report that this is the "beginning of the end" (to quote an eighth grade girl) for them. In other words, this level of math often begins the belief that " I don't totally understand this and therefore I am not good at math." Why an all-girls section? Because single-gender classes have the reported effect of gradually increasing the self-esteem of girls and their beliefs that they can do math.

Constraint — The coeducational cheerleading squad has never had a male member. The internal constraint may be that the boys are afraid of being labeled as "sissies" or "fags."

Remedy — Have a day when the cheerleaders work with the weightlifting class to develop a team cheer that requires great strength. Continue pairing the cheerleaders with various male groups in the school until it becomes ordinary to see males and females doing cheers together.

Anna Quindlen, the Pulitzer Prize-winning journalist, tells a great story about her sons, which illustrates how this works. She was driving home one day with her two boys sitting and talking in the back seat. The oldest boy said to the youngest boy, "I want to be a doctor when I grow up." The youngest boy laughed and said, "You can't be a doctor, doctors are girls." Needless to say, his pediatrician...

External and Internal Constraints

Most situations, when analyzed, have some inequity and there are usually both internal and external constraints operating. It means that it takes longer to do the analysis and requires great thought, creativity, flexibility, and courage to identify and to put effective actions into place. And after all of that, you still have to think through and plan for resistance-lowering strategies.

Let's consider a worst-case scenario: A boys' school has recently turned coeducational. There are four boys for every girl, the faculty is 70% male and the administration is 100% male. Female applicants report that the atmosphere does not feel "comfortable" when they visit the school and only 25% of female visitors actually apply for admission to the school.

All of this data would have been evident after completing a numerical assessment and doing follow-up data collection related to possible causality. The recommended action is to equalize opportunities, remove external constraints, and remove or reduce internal constraints. How does that translate into action?

By now you should be able to see which of these suggestions deal with numerical inequity, external constraints, internal constraints, or any combination of these.

Here goes!

- Hire a consultant.

- Design the admission visits differently for female applicants. For example, have a current female student call her the night before her visit and give her some options of classes to visit, answer questions for her, etc.

- Alter the visual impact of the school. For example, move the hundreds of pictures of male alumni from the front hall to the alumni room.

- Make sure all of the school's literature has female pictures, etc.

- Add a female to the administration (a quick way to do this is to have the female athletic director join the administration).

- Contact area universities and offer to provide field placements, internships, or student teaching opportunities for their female students.

- Invite the area girls' school to participate in theater and social events (Good luck — they'll think you're trying to steal their girls!).

The above list could continue for several more pages. As you think about it, it is really necessary to have two concurrent plans.

Concurrent Plans

First, put into place some fairly easy and inexpensive actions that can alleviate one or more of the issues. If possible, this should be a high visibility, low cost, and popular action. This is the short-term plan (which usually deals with external constraints). It also serves the purpose of getting people on board and interested in the next steps.

At the same time that you are planning the short-term actions, time needs to be spent making a long-term plan. A long-term plan often gets to the causes of issues and works over a period of time to remove or to alter those causes (which often include those change-resistant internal constraints).

A good example of this is a school where far fewer girls than boys take advanced placement math. There are usually many root causes, such as girls who have developed math anxiety or have a low view of their capability, teachers who have not been trained to work with math-anxious or math-challenged girls, a curriculum that is not female friendly, parents who do not do those things that encourage girls to take math, and so on.

The long-term plan would include teacher training, parent education, curriculum analysis, possible single-gender math classes or math support systems for girls, as well as many other possible actions.

It is better to put into action one change that can ameliorate several problems at once. This is so important, I am going to repeat it: *It is better to put into action one change that can ameliorate several problems at once.* Why? Because of the natural tendency of the system to resist change, it is easier to get one thing accepted than to attack with a barrage of changes. It may also be more cost-efficient — and maybe even synergistic.

Strategies to look for are ones with multiple impacts; for example, ones that have a short-term and a long-term impact and that can deal with internal and external constraints. It is the synergy of the two parallel strategies — those that deal with external constraints and those that deal with internal constraints — when combined in an educational system that yield the most powerful effects.

Here are some examples:

- Single-gender classes — powerful short-term results (happier, more satisfied students) and significant long-term results (better grades, test scores, and a higher percentage of students going on to advanced placement courses)

- Mentoring/Modeling — same results as above

- Strengthen self-esteem — see Chapter Three

- Serious and comprehensive teacher training with follow-up video analysis of teachers — not just one gender awareness workshop, but ongoing training in techniques and application, and with teacher review. Videotaping doesn't have to be threatening. It can be done by each teacher and viewed with a trusted colleague (or alone, at home, with a bottle of wine!).

- Direct teaching of gender issues to students — this is very difficult (the affective education movement has been a dismal failure), but not impossible. For instance, you might explain to high school girls and boys about the nerve endings in the face. Since the part of the brain that is related to these sensations of touch is larger in the female brain when compared to the male brain, females prefer a light touch to their face, or a gentle kiss. Boys who have learned about this have altered their kissing behavior. Although this does not sound like critically important gender data, it can be the captivating beginning of a meaningful coeducational conversation that will lead to real understanding, appreciation, and acceptance of gender differences (and similarities).

AAUW Report and Constraints

Stop the presses! Just as the rewrite of this chapter was being completed the AAUW released their newest report, one which the National Science Foundation asked them to conduct, and which looks at the reasons behind the under-representation of women and girls in science, technology, engineering, and mathematics — the so-called STEM areas.

Titled *Why So Few?* This report has the latest in research, paired with specific recommendations and strategies for educators and parents. You can download a copy for free at the AAUW website, and I encourage you to do so — just as soon as you finish reading this book!

This report is replete with examples of, and research on, internal constraints (and a few external ones as well). Some of the highlights:

- Social psychologist, Joshua Aronson, identified "stereotype threat" as the fear of being identified with a negative stereotype, and/or of behaving in a way that confirmed the stereotype. This has a particular strong impact in testing situations, where something as small as being asked your gender before a test, or being one of a smaller number of women than men taking the test, can affect scores. In high importance tests, like the math portion of the SAT, this can mean as much as a 20 point difference. The fear that you will be bad at math because you are a woman becomes a self-fulfilling prophecy. However, when the threat is removed by telling everyone that both sexes perform equally well on a given test, then the women actually perform better than the men!

- Carol Dweck, a social and developmental psychologist at Stanford University, has done research on the difference in attitude and achievement of someone with a "growth mindset" (intelligence is changeable depending on effort) vs. a "fixed mindset" (intelligence is inborn and fixed). This mindset usually doesn't emerge until the individual faces a challenge. In the supportive environment of elementary schools, fixed mindset students usually do fine, but by middle school, with its greater emphasis on independent learning, Dweck finds students about equally divided between the two mindsets.

Dweck first conducted a study to show that students with the growth mindset outperformed those with the fixed mindset. Then she did an additional study to find out what would happen if students were taught that the brain is a muscle that strengthens with use. The students were also taught that mistakes are part of the learning process, and that they control their own learning, so that "being smart is a choice."

Prior to the study, all students had declining grades (not an uncommon result of the transition from elementary to middle school). The students in the control group continued on this downward trajectory. However, the students who were taught the possibility of a "growth mindset" reversed their declining grades!

The AAUW report points out that Dweck's research shows that "for both middle school and college students, a growth mindset protects girls and women from the influence of the stereotype that girls are not as good as boys at math." Therefore, one of the important things that educators and parents can do for girls is to communicate and positively reinforce this idea of a growth mindset. Math is a learned skill, not a gift given at birth.

Along with teaching the growth mindset, it is also important to "highlight the struggle." Or, as Carol Dweck says, "…when you think about a career in science or math or anything, of course you struggle. That's the name of the game! If you're going to discover something new or invent something new, it's a struggle. So I encourage educators to celebrate that, to say: 'Who had a fantastic struggle? Tell me about your struggle!'"

- In my workshops with teachers, I tell them that the brain changes and grows most, both the emotional and rational part, when it struggles, not when something is easy to do or comfortable. I call this "hug the monster." In other words, do what is hard or intimidating. My mother always said, "What doesn't kill you makes you strong." Well, she was a bit prone to hyperbole!

- Because boys are believed to be better at spatial-visualization, which in turn is considered to be essential for success in engineering, Sheryl Sorby, a professor of mechanical engineering and engineering mechanics at Michigan Technological University, developed a course that teaches spatial-visualization skills. After finding success in increasing retention rates of female students in engineering, Sorby ran a pilot study with middle school girls. The girls who took her course took more advanced level math and science courses in high school than the girls who did not. Her class increased their competence, which affected their confidence.

- All of the examples above involve some degree of implicit bias, which by its very nature operates below the conscious radar. Implicit bias is often part of a culture, which may explain why South and East Asian cultures, which believe strongly in the importance of effort (a cultural growth mindset), produce so many more women math and science graduates.

Whether cultural, familial, or personal, implicit bias permeates the messages that educators and parents give their children. It is important, therefore, to identify and understand your biases so that you can develop strategies to compensate for them. A good way to get a start on this is to go to https//implicit. harvard.edu and take one or more of the implicit bias tests that you will find there. As the AAUW report points out, "Educators can look at the effect their biases have on their teaching, advising, and evaluation of students and can work to create an environment in the classroom that counters gender-science stereotypes. Parents can resolve to be more aware of messages they send their sons and daughters about their suitability for math and science."

The Most Critical Internal Constraint for Girls

It is critical that schools educate themselves about all these issues if they are serious about gender equity in the classroom and in the school community. Schools should consider both the external and internal barriers to gender equity. So far, we have focused mostly on the external factors and some of the internal ones.

The most pervasive internal constraint for girls — affecting their choices, their decisions, their aspirations, their achievement, and pretty much everything else — is the pervasive internal constraint of low self-esteem.

This leads us to the next chapter: the self-esteem of girls.

My work over the last thirty years (as well as a vast number of other practitioners and researchers) has documented the progressively downward trend of self-esteem in girls as they move from childhood to tween to teen to young adult. This deteriorating internal factor negatively influences behavior and decision-making in females in a big way.

For females, negative self-esteem is very pervasive. If the self-esteem of girls could be improved, this would have a positive impact on beliefs and behavior. Because all of the external constraints can never be erased in the life of a girl, she needs to *not* have the "double whammy" of the internal constraint of low self-esteem to inhibit her growth.

The self-esteem factor, then, is key to the successful realization of gender equity, female resilience, mental health and motivation. In other words, in the examples given above, girls, whose self-esteem has been heightened, may feel strong and capable enough to speak out in class or to take that advanced placement physics course, or to "hug the monster," regardless of the climate of the classroom or the pedagogical techniques of the teacher.

Girls with low self-esteem can, and probably will, sabotage even the best-laid plans and programs for equitable gender opportunities. Even if a teacher uses such methods as "wait time" to help equalize student input by gender, if the girls in the class do not believe in their capability, they still will not increase their oral input. The key to leveling the gender playing field is a synergistic combination of dealing with the inequitable external constraints while also taking dead aim at the most serious internal constraint: Girls with low self-esteem. This must be done (and it cannot be stressed strongly enough) in a premeditated way over time.

How? Continue on to Chapter Three!

CHAPTER 3
Self-Esteem Is Green

"If you think you can, you can,
And if you think you can't, you're right."
— Mary Kay Ash

Almost all writings about self-esteem or self-concept start with the question: "What do these words mean?" Everyone seems to know the answer, yet the ambiguity of the definitions makes the analysis of problems related to self-esteem more difficult.

One of the best (and shortest) discussions of this problem is contained in the first few pages of *Building Self, Adolescent Girls and Self-Esteem* by Sundra Cee Flansburg. Although it was written in 1993, and is out of print, this is a topic that is not new and the relevance of what Ms. Flansburg has to say hasn't changed. It is an excellent summary of the concept of self-esteem; it's worth the effort to track it down in a library somewhere, so please read it!

Definitions

You may have noticed in this book the more frequent use of the term "self-esteem" over "self-concept." There is good reason for this: Self-esteem implies confidence and satisfaction in oneself, or one's good opinion of oneself. Self-concept, on the other hand, is more neutral, implying something conceived in the mind, a thought or idea of oneself.

When you think about it, everyone has a thought or idea of herself/himself. That may include that I think I am a tomato! Since our stated focus is the internal state that is inextricably tied to emotion and behavior, an evaluative component seems to be needed. Ergo, whether I think I am a good tomato or a bad tomato is more to the point. Therefore, self-esteem is the preferred terminology, since this term includes an evaluative opinion of oneself.

Components of Self-Esteem

Terminology decision made, the next step is to be as specific as possible about the components of self-esteem. If a degree of specificity can be reached, there is hope for creating strategies to facilitate the developing of self-esteem in all students, especially in the population deemed at risk in this area — females.

Everyone who has ever studied, researched, or written about self-esteem has listed several components that blend together to create this internal state; some of these components overlap, some do not. There is more disagreement than agreement about them. In this case we must ask ourselves one question: What are the components, or characteristics, or "things" that, if they were not present, would make it impossible to have positive self-esteem?

At a recent education conference, one teacher suggested that beauty was a component of self-esteem. She must have forgotten about Marilyn Monroe! Certainly feeling positive about your body would be a nice addition, but the litmus test is that you can't have self-esteem without it. Holding various elements up to this light, Porsches, good health, a loving mother, all fall by the wayside. Again, these would be nice additions, but in their absence, many people have very high levels of self-esteem.

So, what are these elusive components?

In the last twenty years of presenting at conferences, I always offer the same three components for the audiences to consider. So far, no one has argued against these as passing the litmus test. There have been arguments for additions, but none for the deletion of one of the big three. That's a very good start. If we can agree on three components, we should be able to combine this with what we know about girls and then develop structures, programs, and opportunities to enhance self-esteem.

Think of self-esteem as having a recipe, such as a cake. If you want the cake to be really good, each ingredient must be included, not too much, not too little. It is the optimum balance of the ingredients that creates the best cake. So, to take this metaphor farther, improvement of, or work on, self-esteem begins first with the analysis of the ingredients. If there is too much of one or not enough of another, the self-esteem cake will be affected. As we will see, then, to improve the cake, sometimes it is a matter of working on the "not enough" ingredient(s) or the "too much" ingredient(s).

Drum roll, please! The three requisite components of self-esteem are:

- Green Frogs
- Green Fingernails
- Green Marbles

The Power of Story

Okay, these are not the actual components, but the titles of stories that represent the components. Why stories and not just a listing? Because brain research suggests that humans tend to remember things better when in context, not in lists; and that stories are a great way to provide that context. An added bonus is that it gives children a concrete, real example to add to the clarity.

Why green? I created these stories for my students when I was a division director at Laurel School and the school's color was green: just another way of making things meaningful to the receivers. One final note, although there is some poetic license involved, the stories come from real life situations.

Green Frogs

Once upon a time there was a little girl names JoAnn. Every summer she and her family would spend several weeks at a fishing camp in the Canadian wilderness, complete with outhouses and black flies.

The summer of her sixth birthday seemed like each summer before it: drive forever, sit in the back seat and get carsick, wake up late at night and board a boat to be transported across the lake to the fishing camp.

All was as expected the next morning. The camp was filled — mostly with men and a few families. All of the children were boys, except JoAnn. She was also the youngest child in the camp again that year. Oh, well. She jumped into the boat with her lunch and her family (mom, dad, nine-year-old brother) for a full day of fishing.

Later that day, as the sun began to set, all of the fishermen, one fisherwoman (JoAnn's mother), and one fishergirl (JoAnn), returned to camp. Although everyone was usually ravenous and wanted to head to the main lodge and the dining room, the tradition was that first the fish had to be cleaned, a hole dug in the deep sawdust of the barn, and the fish laid up against the huge blocks of ice under the sawdust.

The blocks of ice had been cut from the lake in the winter and lasted all summer under the protection of the mountain of sawdust. Every family marked where they had buried their fish with a big stick. Part of the fun was deciding what to put on the stick for identification. JoAnn's family usually chose one of Marty's (JoAnn's brother) socks, since they were quite distinctive with embroidered diamond designs on the ankles (this was, after all, the 1950s).

But on this first night of fishing camp, no one had any fish, except one man. This was quite strange since Healey Lake was famous for its abundance of fish and everyone caught the limit every day. Discussion at dinner that night in the lodge was quite animated. Everyone gathered around the successful fisherman to find out his secret. It didn't take long before it was discovered that he had only used frogs as bait, no worms, no minnows, no lures, only frogs.

As the adults were sitting around and drinking cold Canadian beer (also stored up against the ice, next to the fish, in the barn), the children, as usual, got together to play. But instead of playing, they decided to get into the serious business of figuring out how to cash in on the newly valuable frog market. The plan was to get up very early the next morning and go out and catch as many frogs as possible and sell them to the fishermen, who all left from the main dock at dawn. It would be a great way of adding dimes to the ones used to buy the latest comic books at the lodge.

Frogs like to hunker down in the tall grass right next to the lake. So, it was no mystery where to go frog hunting the next morning. The children fanned out and established their own frog territory and spent the next half hour in serious pursuit of their amphibious victims. Everyone caught some, pretty much in direct correlation to her/his age.

Just as planned, the froggers headed up to the dock, where the fishermen and one fisherwoman were getting their boats ready for the day. Frogs were in great demand and every frogger was sold out of his/her stock within minutes. Marty made a whopping fifty cents, and JoAnn was happy with her dime. After all, she had smaller hands and was not quite as dexterous at frog catching as the older boys.

That night, everyone eagerly headed to the big rock where the fish were cleaned. There were more fish tonight, but the number of fish caught seemed to be exactly analogous to the number of frogs that each fisherman, fisherwoman, or fishergirl had used. And, another startling discovery was made! All of the very large bass or pike that were caught were not caught with just any old frog — they were caught with a "greenie!"

The children shivered, because they instinctively knew that the price of a "greenie" (they got their name from being totally green) would be much higher than just any old regular frog. The problem was that "greenies" were very hard to catch. They have no brown on them like ordinary frogs and were harder to see. Also, they're very skinny, very quick, and seem to have eyes in the back of their heads (since they always see a hand that is about to ensnare them).

No child slept much that night, dreaming of the possible wealth of the next day. Because, before departing to their individual cabins for the night, the children agreed they all needed to charge the same increased price for greenies, thereby being some of the youngest entrepreneurs to engage in price fixing — a "greenie" would cost a quarter tomorrow!

The sun was barely up before the froggers were out skirting the edge of the lake. No one was talking much; the belief was that "greenies" could hear anything. Time went by quickly, because that's what happens when you're chasing "greenies." Just before the boats were ready to depart, the children came running to the dock with their treasures. Everyone, except JoAnn, caught one greenie, and the oldest boy had two. JoAnn knew it was because she was too young to be fast enough to capture a "greenie," but she still felt awful as everyone set off for a long day of fishing.

Dusk arrived, boats returned, fishermen, fisherwoman, and fishergirl all headed to the big rock. Things hadn't changed. This was weird. The fish would bite only on frogs, nothing else, and the largest fish would bite only on the "greenies."

Well, it doesn't take a genius to know that the next day's "greenie" market value was going to be fifty cents. If you're already beginning to feel sorry for JoAnn, don't! She had spent some of her last two mornings not only watching the other froggers, but especially watching the frogs — the green ones. In addition, she got a good deal of sleep that night. Now JoAnn didn't know it, but brain research suggests that if children get enough sleep, their brains "consolidate" what they thought about and experienced the day before (in fact, the latest research shows that even a good nap can have this effect!) So, when JoAnn woke up the next morning, she just knew how to catch greenies!

Just before dawn the froggers tore out of their cabins and headed to the tall grass by the lake. Fishermen and the one fisherwoman began packing the day's necessities in their boats, and soon it was time to leave. The froggers arrived at the docks, breathless.

It was a bad frogging morning, only two "greenies" amongst all of the froggers, but a lot of those ordinary old brown frogs. And then,

JoAnn pushed her way to the front. To everyone's fall-flat-on-your-face astonishment, she had *six* "greenies" in her small bucket and none of those ordinary old brown frogs. JoAnn had a hard time sleeping that night. She said her cheeks hurt from smiling so much all day; plus, she couldn't stop thinking about how much six quarters was!

There is a strategy that is effective to this day for catching green frogs. If you buy this book and write to me, I'll tell you what it is. This is a true story and the names have not been changed to protect the *competent.*

Competence — the first of the three ingredients needed for self-esteem.

Green Fingernails

Since 1896, student volunteering had always been a part of the history of my former school. But in the mid-1990's, interest had waned and the administration was seeking ways of revitalizing this important connection with the larger community. The head of school had heard about the well-known volunteer program at a girls' school in the East and decided to send the two faculty advisors of our emaciated program to visit this school. Off to the East went the school psychologist and the French teacher, both passionate about bringing back the spark that would ignite the students' desire to volunteer. Little did they know that what they would bring back, in addition to that spark, was the knowledge of one of the components of self-esteem.

Denise and JoAnn, the two passionate advisors of the volunteer program, arrived on the campus with enough time to explore other facets of the school and its programs. Denise headed for the French classes. JoAnn headed for the screams she heard coming from the far back part of the campus. Can you tell who was the French teacher and who was the psychologist?

The screams seemed to be coming from a tall collection of rocks that an Ohioan, like JoAnn, would call a small mountain. However, the girls who were there were calling it many other names, most of which cannot be printed here. The focal point of the screams was easy to ascertain upon arrival at the bottom of the mini-cliff. They were issuing from the mouth of a very petite, blond girl who was oh, so nicely dressed, and whose hair was oh, so fashionably styled. She was standing on the top of a rock about seven feet from the ground with a rope tied around her middle. This rope extended to the top of the cliff where a faculty advisor was leaning over the edge saying words of encouragement to the girl below.

The look on JoAnn's face must have been the prompt for a nearby adult to come over and offer an explanation. "You see," she said, "these are the freshmen and this is their on-campus challenge course. All entering ninth graders participate in these activities for the first semester of school while the sophomores, juniors, and seniors go into the city for their weekly volunteer jobs. This is the first challenge. Every girl must make it to the top of the cliff before she is officially a [name of school] girl." Her explanation was cut off by a much louder, longer, even more penetrating scream.

As JoAnn's attention returned to the cliff, the cause of the scream was clear. The girl had moved up the cliff to about ten feet and was sharing her fear and frustration with her advisor at the top. She begged to be let down or pulled up by the rope, and explained convincingly that her muscles were giving out and she was about to faint. Her final wail — "I can't do it!" From up above came the response — "Yes, you can!"

You could almost see the girl calculating what it would take to get someone to rescue her. Then… she let go of the rock. Presumably, she thought if she let go, her advisor would have to haul her up by the rope and she would be done with this horrible challenge.

Well, the previous screams were nothing compared to this one! It must really hurt to have a rope cinched tightly around your waist holding your entire body weight. Have you observed how, in times of crisis, some people notice strange details? Just then JoAnn saw the girl's fingernails — they were very long and nicely shaped, and painted green! She was so focused on the fingernails that she almost missed the look that flashed across the girl's face as she looked up and saw that her advisor was being purposely inattentive to her plight. Surprisingly, her expression seemed to be one of anger. Anger is what we psychologists call one of the most positive of the negative emotions. It tends to promote rapid action.

In the next instant the girl swung herself back to the cliff face, reached out, grabbed the nearest rock and regained her purchase. The cost was one broken green fingernail.

At that point she looked up and seemed to be about to say something, but looked at her advisor's uninterested face and continued to climb. We, the audience at the bottom of the cliff and the audience at the top of the cliff (advisor and some other students), were mesmerized by the display in front of us. She was sweating now, her hair was not so neat, and she was breaking a green fingernail at the rate of one per every three or four vertical feet. But it was her face that was the most riveting.

The previous look of fear and frustration had faded. The closer she got to the top, the more frequently she looked at her advisor. The ground audience was in agreement — her advisor should run for cover before the girl got to the top!

Well, she did get to the top, with every previously perfect green fingernail affected. Faces can be so expressive. No one there will ever forget hers as she gained her footing and looked over the top of the cliff at her vertical route. She looked as if she could climb a real mountain, like one of those monstrous ones in Nepal. She then turned on her heel, headed directly to her advisor and gave her a very long and sincere hug.

The girl's name? I never found out, or she would receive a copy of this book for providing such a great story for the second component of self-esteem — *confidence.*

Confidence — the second of the three ingredients needed for self-esteem.

Green Marbles

Perhaps it was the eels swimming in the small pool in the living room that made them unforgettable. Who really knows? But as we scooped out the eels to save them for dinner later and began to drain the pool, that's when it happened. Marty fell in love. Falling in love is not a strange occurrence usually, but in this case, it bordered on being strange. You see, the object, or objects (to be more precise) of Marty's lustful gaze were large, green marbles. The green marbles lined the bottom of the pool and were responsible for the dazzling green color of the water. My friend, Don, was moving and my nephew, Marty, and I were there to help. We had removed the eels, and drained the pool, now the time had come to remove the marbles. Marty was six years old at the time.

Two years later and several inches taller, Marty came running into the house with a look on his face that was filled with worry. "Aunt JoAnn!" My breathing stopped until his next words tumbled out, "I forgot Carey's birthday party is tonight and I have nothing to take and it starts at seven o'clock and…" I didn't even let him finish. Super Aunt to the rescue!

"Don't worry, Marty, I just got paid, we can swing by the mall, buy a present and have it wrapped and be at Carey's house…" It was his turn to not let me finish. I will never forget the look on his face. Now, twenty years later, I realize that look said, "I love you, Aunt JoAnn, but you are too dumb to live, only I'll tell you that gently." The wise eight-year-old said, "But Aunt JoAnn, that won't mean anything!"

Marty disappeared into the jungle otherwise known as his bedroom and reappeared with a large bucket of green marbles. Yes, Don had given them to him right after he was brave enough to take a bite of eel at dinner all those years ago. The marbles occupied a sacred place by the head of Marty's bed. That way, he could see them before he fell asleep at night and as soon as he woke up in the morning. Love is like that.

"Marty, you love those marbles! Why don't we take half of them and put them in a nice box for Carey?" The same look appeared on his face and I knew he was going to say, "But Aunt JoAnn, that won't mean anything!" I remembered then that his cousin Carey held a special place in Marty's heart. But she was also eight years old, and a girl! We were about to head to a party where Marty would be the only boy and a house full of eight-year-old girls would be "oohing" and "aahing" over each present as Carey opened them one by one.

We were halfway there and I knew I had made a mistake. I should have called Carey's mother and warned her that the somewhat unclean bucket of green marbles was not really green marbles at all, but a bucket of Marty's love. With her prompting, Carey would "ooh" and "aah" over this present along with all the others. But it was too late.

The car stopped, Marty grabbed the bucket of marbles and hobbled into the house as fast as he could with his load. By the time I entered, the newspaper-crookedly-wrapped-by-Marty bucket of marbles sat in the midst of a table full of presents. My worst fears were confirmed. Carey sat in the middle of a horde of girls opening gorgeously wrapped presents. A Barbie doll, barrettes, games and toys were all unwrapped to the sounds of squeals, giggles and smiles. It was obvious that she was saving Marty's present for the very last.

It was time. Carey reached for the large bundle, but could not move it. The other girls helped push it over to her end of the table, while rolling their eyes at the sight of the weird wrapping. I looked at Marty — his eyes were shining with excitement and pride. With a huge smile on her face, Carey ripped open the paper... and the smile promptly disappeared. It seemed like forever before she looked up from the green marbles. With tears in her eyes, she looked at Marty, her voice filled with emotion, and said, "This is the best present I've ever had." I knew then why this girl was so special.

Marty didn't walk to the car, he floated. The next day he tried out for little league baseball and did not make the team. "Oh well, I guess

I'll try soccer." was all Marty said. The aftermath of green marble giving was pretty powerful — the power of *connectedness*.

Connectedness — the third component of self-esteem.

A Word About Connectedness

Connectedness refers to the sense of being a meaningful part of something, to do something meaningful, in essence what I call "out-of-your-own skin experiences." It really refers to the opposite of what many purported self-esteem programs profess.

Self, analysis of self, appreciation of self, are often the core of affective education programs. Focusing on self does not increase self-esteem, but it *can* increase selfishness, a sense of being overly precious, and egocentrism.

Connecting with another human being, feeling a part of a group or community, giving, caring, working for a cause, are all examples of connectedness. It is by focusing outward rather than inward that self is enhanced and becomes the icing on the cake of that word esteem.

Competence, Confidence, and Connectedness

These three C's can't be taught or improved by discussion or self analysis; they must be experienced. It is really the emotion that one feels after "doing" something like

- catching a bucket full of "greenies" and feeling suffused with *competence*

- climbing the cliff and feeling an incredible sense of *confidence*

- watching Cary's joy at your gift of marbles and feeling a wonderful sense of *connectedness*

The key is to analyze which of the ingredients needs to be increased and focus on those activities and behaviors that increase the deficient ingredient. So, we don't work on self-esteem as a whole, but we improve the ingredients that will ultimately lead to a good self-esteem cake. Therefore, adults in the lives of girls need to help structure a girl's world so that she has the opportunities or experiences that will allow her to experience each C "enough" to enhance self-esteem.

If situations are very dramatic, one experience can be powerful enough to change a person forever. A clear example is Outward Bound experiences. Girls who have participated in an Outward Bound experience report a significant change in their self-esteem. More often, experiences need to be layered over time, like a strudel.

In thinking about the three C's, it is important to keep in mind that the balance and synergy between them is critical to the development of self-esteem. All three need to be present and somewhat equal to yield the highest levels of self- esteem.

For example, the person who has a high level of connectedness but much lower levels of confidence and competence will be less likely to take risks or to face conflict than if there are high levels of all three C ingredients. This person can be susceptible to peer pressure, open to being a victim, care about pleasing to the exclusion of self-interest or self-preservation, and so on.

This approach not only gives you a very critical diagnostic measure of self-esteem, but it also provides a guide for deciding strategies for enhancing self-esteem. Therefore, if a person is low in competence, strategies and programs need to be made available that will develop this person's competence in a meaningful way.

Hugging the Monster

One clear example of this is math anxiety in girls. Math anxiety in girls is most often the result of a lack in both confidence and competence and the synergism is the double whammy. If I don't feel confident enough to try something that isn't immediately clear to me, I won't do it as much, and over time, that makes me feel incompetent. This is especially true in a class where many boys don't hesitate to try, fail, and keep going until they get it. That is why being in an all-girls' math class for a year or two has such magic effects. The girls hesitate less to struggle when there are many who are struggling together and the atmosphere is more cooperative. This leads to greater confidence that then leads over time to greater competence. In other words, "hugging the monster" allows a girl's confidence to grow and leads to growing competence. These two C's will allow her to stick with something that is a real challenge for her.

Why Math?

This may be a good place to explain why math examples and concerns are a central focus of this book. Consider these points:

- Colleges and universities are positively influenced by applicants who take, and do well in, advanced placement math courses or tests. Ergo, admission is impacted significantly regardless of the major area of interest of the applicant.
- Most predictions of employment opportunities for the future indicate that our technologically based world will require extensive background and knowledge in math.
- The AAUW study (*Shortchanging Girls, Shortchanging America*) showed a significant correlation between a female's perception of her mathematical skills and her self-esteem. This correlation did not exist with any other subject area.

It is important that girls are offered a strong educational program in all academic areas (including the arts and physical education, which have solid support from the brain research) — and that their individual strengths and interests are encouraged. Taking this into account it is still essential for girls to do as much math as possible.

Another Word About Connectedness (and about oxytocin as well)

Connectedness poses a special problem for girls, because girls produce a hormone called oxytocin, which has been labeled the "tend and befriend" hormone in the popular literature. One of oxytocin's pervasive, and lifelong effects, is the drive to care about others and to have others care about us. In my parlance, girls are neurobiologically primed to have a higher need (and want) in this area. It can often lead to the three C's being lopsided: too much connectedness.

The "double whammy" happens when this high connectedness need is combined with low confidence and competence. This means schools must have programs and opportunities for girls not only to increase competence and confidence, but also refocus some of what I call the "connectedness needs" to something other than peers or boyfriends.

In my work, I have found that girls who spread out the need for connectedness by belonging to a group outside of school, or a team, or tutoring others or, taking care of animals, etc., have eased the pressure of fulfilling this high need from one source: a friend, a clique or a boyfriend. In many ways this spreading of connectedness helps keep them healthy and balanced when the peer and friendship issues start to rock and roll a girl's boat.

What To Do

To figure out how to help a girl increase her self-esteem, she and the adults in her life need to do an analysis of the three C's. Then, they need to think of which "doing" opportunities or behaviors, once experienced, would begin to increase a particular ingredient. Finally, for the sake of efficiency and effectiveness, it makes sense that those programs that affect all three C's would be the most powerful and yield the most significant impact.

Let's take a look at four educational programs that are fairly popular as a result of the recent gender research. All of these programs have the potential to increase all three C's. Unfortunately, many are not structured or planned adequately enough to realize this power and the outcome is left to serendipity.

Mentoring

Connectedness — By their very nature, mentoring programs provide opportunities for participants to experience connectedness (being a meaningful part of something or someone other than self). The problem with many mentoring programs is that they are too short-term, or are "one-shot" opportunities and do not allow the full development of connectedness.

Programs that extend over a year or more tend to have more long lasting effects in connectedness and, subsequently, self-esteem. The dorm programs for female math majors at several universities are an example of this. Other good examples are programs that connect girls with professionals in fields of interest to the girls. If a middle school girl wants to be an artist, for example, then she is connected with an adult artist in the community and the two of them have the opportunity to interact together many times over a several year period.

Competence — This component is not necessarily a part of many mentoring programs and needs to be deliberately planned and inserted. In one public school in Warren, Ohio, computer experts from a local business come into the school over a period of a year and teach their "mentees" (all elementary school students) how to use the computers that their company has donated to the school.

Confidence — Although this can be the by-product of experiences that lead to competence, it cannot be taken for granted that this *will* happen. It needs to be a planned part of the mentoring experience. To take the above example, mentors could train their mentees in using a software program, to memorize math facts, and to work with them until this is an automatic skill and they can get an A on a timed math fact quiz.

Confidence is something that almost magically forms from connectedness, competence, and doing, or using, the newly formed competence.

A caveat: although male mentors can be effective working with girls, the modeling that female mentors provide simply by showing that someone of that gender can be a success, is a powerful confidence booster.

Challenge Courses
(Outward-Bound type experiences)

Connectedness — A group that works together over a period of time to overcome a common obstacle connects around that struggle. It is as simple and as complex as that. Whether you have filled sand bags to save your hometown from a flood, or just lived through a rope course together, it works. There is some validity to the statement that the more serious, difficult, or dangerous the task, the deeper the connectedness. Just look at recent cases of flooding and earthquakes that have coalesced rescuers from all over the world to work with local communities.

Competence — Because of their very nature, challenge courses provide the opportunity to build competence. Learning from each other, failing and trying again, developing strategies that work are all part of this.

Confidence — Please re-read the green fingernail story, there is no need to say more here.

Many challenge courses are individually based. This works particularly well if the person involved is low in competence or confidence. If connectedness is also an issue, individual challenge courses obviously do nothing to improve this.

For institutions, trying to achieve the highest gain for the most people for the least cost means that group challenge courses are more effective than individual courses. For those individuals who are not athletically or physically talented, there are challenge courses that rely on thinking skills and group interdependence that accomplish the same goals.

Cooperative Learning

Connectedness — Although it is often assumed that cooperative learning techniques fulfill the requisite for connectedness (which is one of the main reasons they are recommended for girls) this is not necessarily the case. The experiences need to be structured in such a way that the participants of the group will interact in a positive way and the structure of the task is such that everyone will participate. This is no easy feat!

A class that is told to form groups of four and find the answer to a physics problem or to discuss the role of a character in a novel often fail to achieve connectedness. The group needs to be balanced to promote interaction with not too many leaders or too many followers.

The balance of gender in the formation of cooperative groups needs to be a consideration also. Given the literature indicating the possibility of gender inequity in a coeducational setting, there may need to be guidelines or work rules to ensure better equity. For example, the note-taking function needs to rotate, each participant needs to be responsible for a part of the project, etc. Dominance by gender, personality or talent destroys the power of increasing connectedness in a group setting.

Competence — The same is true for achieving this component; that is, learning tasks need to be structured so that the members of the group will become more competent because of working together. This often means putting a diverse group of learners/performers together so that the strong suit of each learner combines to create a powerful group effect.

Confidence — If the above two C's are realized, the probability of the group members becoming more confident is greatly increased, but not always. Continuing work with the same group, repetitive experiences, rehearsals, etc. all work together to increase the confidence of the group and need to be embedded in the cooperative learning experience. Group confidence, over time, generalizes to individual confidence.

Effective cooperative learning experiences for all members of the group are extremely difficult to achieve, which is why many teachers try, but do not continue with, this approach. It requires knowledge of how to form effective groups, how to define tasks that require the participation of every student in each group, and how to carefully monitor the work of the groups. But don't give up; with some additional reading and experimentation, most teachers report powerful changes in attitude and productivity in students in a cooperative learning environment.

Single-Gender Classes, Groupings, or Experiences

Connectedness — The research suggests that, with boys removed, the females in the class, or activity, become more interactive and comfortable. This experience over time leads to a sense of connectedness within the group, through helping one another, listening to, and accepting each other's points of view, and all the other aspects of interaction.

Competence — This component often follows in an all-female group because of the sense of comfort and willingness to take risks. In addition, because teachers are now free to change their pedagogical techniques to better fit the needs of females, there is a corresponding increase in the competence of the girls.

Confidence — From the literature, this seems to be the most common and immediate effect of single-gender experiences. Girls report that they are more confident about talking, tackling problems, and expressing their ideas. Therefore, it does not seem to be necessary to plan for the development of confidence, but merely to provide the opportunity of a single-gender educational experience for it to arise. However, even in all all-girls' environment, the climate of trust and acceptance needs to be fostered, keeping teasing to a minimum and adopting a zero tolerance for "put downs."

A Word About Assigned Seating

One final recommendation for all types of programs and classes: minimize free-seating and use assigned seats almost all of the time. Assigned seats should be changed every few weeks or with a new unit or project. Why? From as early as age four or five, most girls show tendencies of what I call "glomming on" to a few girls or friends and excluding most others. Why does this matter? There are many reasons, but I'll just focus on two.

First, universities and employers are looking for people who have the ability to get along with and interact with a wide variety of people in this very connected and global world. If girls are mostly given the choice of who to sit by or who to work with, their band of choice remains narrow. But, having to work with, sit by, interact with everyone in a class or a school over periods of weeks and months and years, changes not only a girl's band of acceptance of types of people, but also her skill in interacting with a much wider range of humans. I call this *expanding the band*. It expands her band of inclusiveness and reduces her band of exclusiveness.

Second, interacting with a range of classmates will expand a girl's band of social savvy-ness: her ability to understand and interact effectively with a wide variety of human beings. For more justification of the need to "expand the band," read: *A Whole New Mind*, by Daniel H. Pink or *Five Minds for the Future*, by Harold Gardner, or watch the video on youtube.com: *Shift Happens*.

The Big Four

Mentoring, challenge courses, cooperative learning, and single-gender opportunities are the Big Four when it comes to impact on girls, their sense of self, and their level of achievement. These four have shown the most significant impact on the self-esteem, and resultant behavior and performance, of girls. Many other similar strategies are available and important in the overall planning of programs and techniques for gender equity.

It really is a matter of taking the time and effort required to analyze a system thoroughly, to make a comprehensive plan to develop equitable programs that will remove or reduce both external and internal constraints, and to put those plans into effect. It sounds so simple. It is a long, hard and very rewarding process.

CHAPTER 4

Crucible Moments, Crucible Events

Every interaction a child has during the course of a day helps form the adult that child will become. — JoAnn Deak

We know that gender inequities exist. We know that schools need to look carefully at their programs and practices to uncover (and remove) the barriers to equitable education. We know that self-esteem is the key to success in school for girls. We know what programs help build self-esteem in girls. So what's left — the experience of everyday life.

The question for this chapter is: What is important for parents and educators to think about and to do during the formative years to help foster the development of healthy and strong girls?

In order to answer this question, what advice is succinct yet specific enough, wise yet practical enough, simple enough to put into practice, but complex enough to have a lasting effect?

Succinct and simple come first. One of the best ways to illustrate this is with the strudel theory. Strudel? Yes, strudel.

Strudel Theory

Creating a strudel is very much like the recipe for putting together, over time, the development of a healthy and strong child. All of us are the accumulation of genetic material intricately combined with the impact of environmental experiences layered over time — like filo dough in a strudel.

Basic strudel theory says that the critical core of parenting and educating is to think with premeditation and care, planning those experiences that, in small increments, over days, weeks, months, and years help layer and build the child. That is why the first thing you see in this chapter and on my website is this quote — "Every interaction a child has during the course of the day helps form the adult that child will become."

Do I really mean that every little experience, every second of being and of responding to a child as a parent or teacher is critical? Well, yes, to a degree.

The good news is that children, who basically feel loved and are part of an environment that feels relatively safe and consistent, can withstand many adult missteps with little or no lasting negative effects. Examples include the teachable moments that didn't get handled particularly well or the many parental mistakes that are bound to occur, regardless of good intentions.

Although parenting is often serendipitous and reactive to things like how much sleep your daughter had the night before and therefore, her level of crankiness the next day; that is not the substance of this chapter. It is our response to the crucible events or moments that is the focus here. It is critical for all of us to think about our responses in terms of child development and how our responses can be part of layering the strudel in positive ways. With the wrong approach, we can impede the development of self-esteem. With the right approach we can help self-esteem to continue to grow and thrive.

Crucible Moments/Events

How crucible moments/events are handled is critical.

Let's take a brief, general tour of the human brain. The cortex, the big pecan-like structure with hemispheres, is the rational part of the brain. It thinks and it remembers. Deep in the lower brain is a structure called the amygdala. It feels and it remembers. The combination of the two of these brain structures help us to learn, adapt, remember critical events, and be guided by our thoughts and emotions, not just in the present, but the future also. That means that we are meant to remember and be influenced by events and our emotional reactions to them. So, when a dog bites a girl, that moment is captured in thought and feeling causing an immediate reaction (run or cry) and a long-term effect (avoidance of dogs or fear of large hairy animals).

Memory of very high emotions gets chemically burned into a structure called the hippocampus, deep in the brain. Once a memory is stored there, it is very difficult to attenuate. Most professionals in the brain field believe that this structure was designed for species survival and, therefore, can be quite influential on future behavior. That leads to another pattern that has been identified: negative emotions are often stored more frequently and for a longer period of time than positive emotions.

I often use this in my workshops on bullying. I say to girls, be mean once and the girls will probably remember it forever. Be nice ten times afterwards and that not only will not erase the mean behavior memory, but it also won't be remembered as long.

The reason the development of self-esteem is so critical in girls is that they need to be as sturdy and resilient as possible to handle the moments and events in their lives that are not always conducive to keeping their self-esteem at a healthy high. So, yes we need to teach girls how to catch green frogs and how not to care if (occasionally) they break a fingernail freshly painted with beautiful green nail polish. And, yes, they need to experience how important it is to give a treasured bucket of green marbles to someone else.

The premeditated arranging of these experiences over time is critical to the long-term development of the self-esteem of children. But life also happens to us, regardless of our planning. So, in addition to layering the doing of such things in the lives of children, we need to think how we should react when these life events occur spontaneously.

I refer to experiences that are profoundly influential in the life of a girl as being crucible. Crucible events and moments are what help forge a human being. Events are those big happenings like the death of a parent or divorce or being moved to a new school when you have just found your niche in your present school. For girls, many crucible events occur in these areas:

- Discipline
- Risk-taking
- Change
- Loss/Separation
- Friendship

A picture may be worth a thousand words, but in terms of understanding human beings, a story must be worth a million! Lois story captures the essence of the issues related to crucible event #1 — discipline.

Crucible Event #1 — Discipline

Lois was sent to my office because she had defaced school property, which in this case meant that she had written a negative statement on the classroom wall about her second-grade homeroom teacher. No one had seen her do this, but it happened right after Lois did not get chosen to speak during any of the reading class time (talking to an audience was one of her favorite things to do). Everyone could tell that Lois was not happy. Also, handwriting analysis of the wall missive did not require an expert's skill to recognize the distinctive penmanship that was Lois'.

For reasons that we can only speculate on at this time, Lois seemed to have experienced discipline as synonymous with punishment. So, when Lois walked into my office, she had "the look" which basically meant, "I'm innocent and I will lie through my teeth to prove it to you." She was braced and ready for the onslaught.

But discipline is not synonymous with punishment according to the strudel theory of human development, and this was a crucible event.

Lois sat down and composed her face into the pained innocent-about-to-be-accused look. "Lois," I said, "do you remember when you got in a fight on the playground when you were in kindergarten and you explained to me that you hit that person because she had done something bad to someone else? You were so upset about what you considered to be bad behavior on the part of the other girl that you didn't care about breaking the school rule. So, you told the truth about hitting, even though you knew you would get into trouble for doing that.

"Then, I remember the time when you came to tell me that you didn't think it was fair that only new students were given school pens when they came to school for new students' orientation, and their assigned buddies, who took them around the school on that day, didn't get one. Again, I was impressed that you had the courage to tell me, even though I am the director here, that you thought I was doing something that wasn't fair. I've always admired you because you try to be honest even when it is scary for you. Now you're here, and you're scared because you know I have to punish the person who wrote something unkind on the wall about Mrs. Carr."

To make a very long story much shorter, this strategy of acknowledging Lois' basic nature, of setting the tone that she is respected and that this would be not only about punishment, seemed to be helpful, but not sufficient. She lied and denied that her hand and her writing instrument had been instrumental in the finished product on the wall.

So, I had to add the clean-slate part. "I have a terrible memory," I told her, "and after we settle this episode, in the future when I see you, none of this will be left in my memory. I won't think of you or remember you as someone who had been sent to my office for doing something against the school rules." It worked: the tears and words started tumbling simultaneously. We decided on the punishment, and I especially knew it had all worked when she turned as she left the room to ask if my memory problem had kicked in yet!

What is this all about? Well, girls, especially

- respond to disciplinary issues with the moral orientation of connectedness and caring. Lois needed to know that two adults (in this case the teacher and the director) whom she cared about, would not think she was a terrible person because of what she had done

- will learn to be secretive if they hear consistently that they should be "good girls" who never do anything inappropriate

- will stop translating their anger and frustration into more appropriate and healthier behavior if they are only punished and not guided to find direct ways of communicating their concerns

This story also highlights the importance of understanding how this relates to the three C's paradigm:

- Lois's walking out with improved *confidence* knowing she could handle a very difficult situation

- Our discussion of strategies for talking to her teacher directly or writing a note to her about her anger, thereby improving her *competence* to handle future bouts of anger or frustration in a more effective way

- Her feelings of *connectedness* and caring had started out as a hindrance to telling the truth. Our long conversation helped her understand that this connectedness, being trusted and respected, would not be impaired because she made a misstep.

A Word About "Missteps"

It seems to be especially important to use this type of word, "misstep" instead of being bad or doing something wrong. It also lets children know that missteps are part of learning and growing and not held against them in a moral way. Remember Carol Dweck's research in Chapter Two and her emphasis on the value of "the struggle." It is important for children to know that missteps are part of the process of learning and growing.

In fact, one of the newest findings of the brain research is that there is a part of the brain that is activated when we make a misstep. It is called the anterior cingulated gyrus or the "mistake filter." It seems that learning and memory are enhanced somewhat by the power of the mistake filter. In simple terms, the brain seems to have been designed to learn more and remember more when we make a misstep compared to doing something perfectly right the first time. In my workshops, I have begun to underscore the importance of encouraging girls to try things without being able to do them perfectly, not being undone when we do something "wrong," but adjusting and moving on with life. As you can imagine, this concept of the importance of learning by making mistakes has huge ramifications for the tendency of girls to lean towards perfectionism.

Strudel theory: if parents and other significant adults keep in mind the layering of the three C's during experiences of discipline, a very healthy strudel (er, girl), will be the end result. Once is not enough. Luckily children keep making missteps (as do adults) so that it seems that we have more than adequate opportunities to respond with guidance as the major component of discipline, and punishment as a needed, but minor, component.

Crucible Event #2 — Risk-taking

It's important to define risk-taking. It means so many different things to different people and often a personal definition can lead to misunderstandings in this crucible event. In psychological terms, risk-taking involves doing something outside of one's emotional comfort zone. If climbing a cliff is exhilarating and not scary, it is not really risk-taking for that individual. It may be a risk in terms of getting hurt physically, but it is not risk-taking behavior in the classic psychological view. It is the psychological or emotional risk-taking that has such profound influence on strudel building.

In this case, our instructor is Lauren, a fourth-grader.

Gymnastics is an important part of the P.E. curriculum throughout the lower school years because of its effects on positive body image, control, muscle development, and movement through space. Doing a backwards mid-air somersault is one of the milestones set in the gymnastics curriculum. This was always Lauren's Achilles heal.

Each year she would face gymnastics season with some dread and fear, but also with some grit. She had been trying to do this gymnastics feat ever since she was in the first grade — a difficult move for any elementary school child. One of the challenges for Lauren was that she was not as lithe as most gymnasts. But every year, when the gymnastics unit started, she would take out her portfolio and write down her goal for the year — a backwards mid-air somersault. Each year she would work so hard, each year she would come a bit closer. Each year she failed and was glad to move on to baseball season.

Fourth grade was the last year in the primary division. The gymnastics unit ended with a show for all of the primary parents and students. Every grade level did something. However, the highlight of the show was the individual performances by each fourth grader.

Lauren had been dreading this for four years. And yet, to everyone's surprise, Lauren chose to do a routine that had a part at the end where she went to the corner of the full floor mat, ran catty-corner across it, and at the midsection of the mat leapt into the air with a backwards somersault. Her P.E. teacher made sure Lauren knew, that even at the last minute, she could change this to an on-the-mat backwards somersault (which was what she ended up doing in each of the practices).

I had missed seeing the rehearsal where Lauren had completed everything correctly except the somersault. So, when Lauren went to the mat to start her routine and was waiting for the music to start, I had no idea why the tension in the room was so palpably high, or why Miss Wilson (her P.E. teacher for the past four years) was leaning forward, or why every single fourth grade girl sat bolt upright.

The routine was very nice. Lauren was obviously giving it her all. I thought it was merely her way of putting a good ending on her elementary gymnastics stint. Then, the music had a brief pause. Lauren stood poised at the end of the mat, the music started up again, she began running across the mat, she went up in the air, the entire fourth grade and Miss Wilson went up in the air, too. Lauren did the backwards somersault in mid-air and came down with a perfect landing. I was startled when thirty-five fourth graders and one P.E. teacher all screamed, "Yes!" simultaneously and then proceeded to rush to the center of the gym, and with no words or planning, lifted Lauren on their shoulders and carried her around the gym. It wasn't until the teary Miss Wilson told us the background story that we understood what we had witnessed.

Late that day, at lunch, I explained to Lauren why she was one of my role models, because she never gave up trying to do something that mattered to her, even though it was very difficult. At the end of the year, she wrote me a note that said her "heart had filled up like a balloon" when everyone screamed "yes," and when I told her she was one of my role models, and that she would never forget that day, ever, no matter how long she lived. I made a point of talking to her again to tell her that everyone would have reacted the same, yelled "yes," carried her on their shoulders, and I would have told her she was one of my role models, even if she had fallen and not had a perfect landing. It took her awhile to understand that.

Important components of this experience, layered over four years:

- No one ever said to her that this might be too hard, that she might want to try a somersault on the ground, or that her body was not the best designed for a somersault in flight.

- She felt supported, not deflated, when she was not able to meet her goal right away.

- The goal was not set for Lauren by someone else.

- She was taught how to break up this skill into its component parts and to master each part over time. An important contribution to this was a video camera that all of the girls used to tape their work which they critiqued with their peers and teachers after each class.

- Her parents supported her gymnastics dream by paying for gymnastics lessons even though they knew she would never go to the Olympics as a gymnast.

Competence and *confidence* were intricately connected to high expectation under conditions of great nurturing and support.

What is sometimes pejoratively called "the Little League" parent is the obverse of this: someone who sets the bar very high, minus the nurturing conditions. This is often the root issue when female athletes who are Olympic hopefuls burn out and quit at a very young age.

As the research would predict, high expectations without support are more deleterious for females than males. I call this the *magic blend*: an environment, family or situation that has a good balance of caring and challenge. This blend is what gets the most out of a girl. The connectedness factor is also fairly apparent in this story. Lauren may have been literally lifted into the air by her classmates after the somersault, but their *connectedness* to her and hers to them helped lift her figuratively into the air for the somersault.

Crucible event #3 — Dealing with Loss or Separation

There are many examples in this category that move along a continuum from the separation of a preschooler from a parent on the first day of school, to the divorce of parents, to the death of a beloved grandparent and all of the permutations and combinations in between. Irene's story taught all of us a great deal about the more traumatic end of this continuum.

It's hard for us to remember, as adults, what is joyous about being a seven-year-old, until you spend time with a seven-year-old like Irene. She would burst through the front door of the school and beg to be allowed in the classroom early because "Mrs. G." was waiting for her. And, it was true, Mrs. G., her second grade homeroom teacher, like all of Irene's homeroom teachers through the years (she had been at the school since she was three), often encouraged her to come to the classroom early because she filled it with such energy and excitement and movement and chatter. What a way for a teacher to start the day!

So, it was with terrible pain and sadness that winter that we began to have meetings to talk about how to be supportive to Irene, her family, and all of us at the school who had become part of her extended family. Her mother was getting close to ending her battle with cancer, an end that would leave Irene without the presence of her mother in this world.

The first faculty meeting was one of "shoulds." We should make sure she would meet with the school psychologist so that she could talk about her feelings. We should make sure that she could go to the nurse at any time. We should make sure that she was relieved from doing her homework and did not feel pressure about what she had to learn at school. We should send a note home to the other parents in the class so that when Irene went to their homes for play days they would know what was going on at home for Irene. The list went on.

It was a very useful first meeting. It led to our thinking through, as a school, how best to respond to this crucible event in the life of a child in a way that not only was supportive, but also helped the child to face her future life a bit stronger. That's when we threw the "shoulds" out of one of the school windows and began another conversation.

Irene's mother would talk only to Mrs. G. (luckily they had been friends before Irene was born). That formed our first guideline: Irene's mother could not handle talking to many people, including the director of the lower school, so Mrs. G. was the communication liaison.

The next step was to talk to Irene and her father, to see what they needed us to be, and how best to proceed in providing that.

Dad asked for some reading materials. Irene asked that her school day be untouched: that her school remain a safe place where not many people knew about her mother's deteriorating condition, that no one talk to her with a tone of sympathy, that no exceptions for schoolwork be made for her, and that she did not want to talk to our psychologist.

We learned a great deal that year.

After Irene's mother died, we talked with all of the second graders about how Irene wanted us to act when she came back to school. We also shared with the girls the traditional psychological wisdom about how to express their thoughts and feelings to Irene with letters that she could read outside of school where she had the time and space to deal with them, but not to talk to her about this topic at school, unless Irene initiated it.

We met with the parents of her friends to have the same conversation. Much of this happened with the permission and approval of Irene's dad, but not with Irene's knowledge. Her family felt strongly that it would bother Irene if she knew, at that time, that we were talking about her and her grief with her friends and their families; that she would feel watched and so different from the other girls and that would add to her stress, not reduce it.

Two years later, Irene's father remarried and they had plans to move to a new house. We learned even more from Irene's stepmother. She came in to talk about how best to help Irene with the transition of moving from where she had been raised, in a home decorated and lived in by her mother, to a new place. We talked about the importance of consulting with Irene and asking her if taking part of her home and her mother to her new home was important to her. It was.

Irene's new home has the flowers lining the driveway — all the way up to the front door — that Irene's mother had planted at her previous house. They were lovingly dug up and transferred there by Irene and her stepmother.

There is no blueprint for responding to death and dying, an incredible crucible event in the life of a child. Each approach needs to be designed somewhat individually. Irene has grown, physically and emotionally — she is an adult now.

What are the salient features of how Irene's loss was handled?

- There is little traditional wisdom, and we need to be very careful not to impose our emotional needs or psychological history on the situation. That's what the first faculty meeting was all about. Being careful not to be pushed by our baggage of "shoulds" or what made *us* feel better was exceedingly difficult for the adults in her life.

- *Competence* is a key factor. Irene needed to have part of her life with untouched expectations so that she could continue to perform and to be normal. Again, the first reaction of the adults in her life was to lower the bar, so to speak, to make things easier for her. It would have made things so much harder. School was a kind of sanctuary. She was hurting so badly, she just needed her school to be a place to set that aside as much as possible and be the Irene she always had been, not the Irene-who-just-lost-her-mother.

- There are multiple examples of *connectedness* in the above story. Irene's connectedness to the school and to her teacher played a huge role in maintaining a healthy path through this time period.

- It was the relationships that were important. At some points, this caused confusion as adults and other children tried to use the material world to assuage Irene's pain — buying her wonderful presents, constantly taking her places or doing things so that she wouldn't think about her mother.

- Connectedness and competence are interrelated factors in terms of Irene being consulted about her needs and then helping to design the process. There is also a limit to this, as shown by our decision to talk to Irene's friends, even though we knew that she would have vetoed that decision. The judgment center of the brain (the prefrontal cortex) is not fully-grown until at least the early 20s. So, there is always a balance of how much input in decision-making a child/adolescent gets to have. Of course, every parent struggles with where that line is most healthy and effective.

All of the above resulted in the increasing *competence* of Irene and her family to cope with pain and loss and will be translated to her increasing capability to handle future crucible events in her life.

Crucible Event #4 — Dealing with Change

Change is certainly part of loss and separation as discussed above. But change, in and of itself, is also a major component of everyone's life. Enter Abbey.

Abbey's parents made an appointment to talk about whether or not Abbey should come to our school in September. Even though they had already signed a contract and paid their deposit they were concerned because — although Abbey was only four years old — she had experienced eight major changes in her life, including several geographic, school, house, and family pattern changes.

Mom explained that Abbey was presently attending an area nursery school, where she could remain next year, but the family was so impressed with our school that when an opening occurred, they jumped at the chance. They were now having second thoughts, especially since their pediatrician had just told them that a great deal of change was very stressful for children.

Their question: should they keep her at her present school to reduce the amount of change in her life, or should they move her to our school in September, where they hoped she would stay until graduation from high school?

I asked them to describe Abbey to me.

What followed was the story of a child who had loving parents, a safe and consistent home environment (although the actual physical structures changed a bit!), a nurturing and interesting school environment (although, again, there had been a few different ones), and no evidence of symptoms of stress. Abbey laughed a lot, looked forward to going to school, liked people and talked easily to strangers, slept well, and ate well.

Mom talked about all the things she and her husband had done to help with the transitions and to keep connections. Abbey had pictures of all of the schools and houses she had lived in, she called the children from her previous neighborhoods, her bedroom in each new house had the same furniture and the walls were painted the color of Abbey's choice (which they planned and talked about before each move).

Without really knowing why or how, Abbey's parents had the wisdom and intuition to deal with the how of these crucible change events in ways that were growth-producing. They had layered these experiences in such a way that Abbey had become an adaptive and competent human being who valued her past, present, and future connections.

I explained that it was not the quantity or the timing of change that was "bad" for children, but how it was structured and handled. In their case, it really didn't matter whether Abbey stayed at her present school or came to our school; they had created the layering of the filo dough so that they were going to have a healthy strudel no matter which choice they made.

This crucible event underscores so clearly that there are no experiences in and of themselves that are all bad or all good. It isn't the what of human development, it is the how. Change is not bad. But change handled ineffectively can have many negative effects.

Abbey's parents thought about how to make sure that her three C's would be enhanced by all the changes in her life. She was incredibly *connected* to her parents, who stayed a constant in the midst of all of the external changes in her life. She obviously felt safe and comfortable enough because of this constancy to learn how to meet and interact with new people, thereby steadily increasing her *competence* and *confidence* over time. Abbey's parents also used tricks of the psychological trade such as making her bedroom look and feel the same regardless of the city in which it may have been located.

One caveat needs to be added here. Abbey also had the good fortune to have a temperament that allowed her to benefit from her parents good sense and planning. There are some children who are born with a temperament that immediately rails against any amount of change, no matter how well it is handled. But we can't negate the importance of how change is handled just because it is easier or harder for some than others.

What are the salient issues surrounding change:

- The very essence of change is that it disrupts the status quo. Therefore, all change requires some adjustment and care.

- There is a continuum of temperament that responds to change, from what I call worrier to duck. A worrier needs much more support, preview of changes, more gradual change strategies, etc. A duck seems able to let everything roll off of her back, to be less bothered by change and actually seems to respond positively to changes and diversity. With a girl with this latter type of temperament, preparing her for change will be much easier. In either case, having some input in what, when, or how change is happening helps most girls handle change better. Giving a girl some sense of control is important.

Crucible Event #5 — Issues of Friendship

As you are well aware by now, friendship is a critical component in the lives of most females, and therefore, provides rich opportunities for crucible events/moments. How we handle these moments as wise adults in the lives of developing girls is the gist of Dana and Molli's story.

Dana and Molli had both been conscientious students all year. They truly loved their teacher, Miss Crissman, so they gave all of their academic tasks their best efforts. However, once they started to become friends and to spend time together, things changed. Their interest in each other seemed to supersede schoolwork. Some assignments weren't completed on time. Dana and Molli were late for science class and were found in the rest room talking and giggling.

They almost made it through to summer without any serious incidents. But then, with only six days to go, Miss Crissman escorted both Dana and Molli to my office. Their offense was making fun of another classmate (who had a newly acquired bump on her nose due to an accident) and causing that classmate to cry.

I asked Miss Crissman to leave and, uncharacteristically (I want very much for it to be true that I acted uncharacteristically), began to share my disappointment with their recent behavior without listening to a word they had to say. I then said I needed to think about this and sent them on their way.

Afterwards, I watched them march down the hall, muttering all the way, "It's not fair." Meaning of course that how I handled the situation was not fair. It is so hard on adults when children are right and we are wrong!

Later that day, I called the girls' mothers to let them know why their daughters might come home and say that they were sent to the director's office. Dana's mother listened very politely and intently to what happened. And then she had what can be described as a typical, knee-jerk parental reaction. She said that Dana had invited Molli for a play day that weekend and she would cancel that event, since, obviously, the nature of their friendship was causing both of them to behave inappropriately and therefore, this was not a "positive friendship."

Her response elicited the going-against-the-grain spiel. I explained that there is a very important process in social development which is crucial for us as adults to try not to interfere with or to control — no matter how tempting. Girls of this age need the freedom to sample friendships, trying different sizes, types, intensities, and flavors. A bit like trying all of Baskin-Robbins' thirty-one flavors of ice cream before knowing which flavor is the best.

It is important to make mistakes at a fairly young age and to choose some pretty yucky flavors, I explained. If we're lucky girls will make choices early in life that result in things like being sent to the director's office. If they make "poor" choices later, it could result in much worse consequences like becoming pregnant or taking drugs.

If parents try to control friendships early, only allowing play dates with sterling friendship options, girls will not learn about the diversity of human nature and the best fit for them in terms of a more lasting relationship. By the time we finished our conversation, Dana's mother was thanking her lucky stars that Dana wanted to spend time with Molli on Saturday.

So it was back to the drawing board with Molli and Dana. The next day both came to my office, at my invitation, to hear what the consequences would be for their actions. This time I asked them to tell me their version of what had happened.

They began by denying vehemently that they intentionally hurt the feelings of the owner of the bicycle-accident-induced-lumpy-nose. Instead, "lumpy nose" was telling the story and laughing about it herself, and they just joined in, but would not have wanted to hurt her feelings — she was a friend! To the other charges, they pleaded guilty, acknowledging that their new friendship was sometimes more fun and seemingly more important than school work or being on time to science class. They promised never to let their friendship interfere with their focus on school again; and were now ready for the dire consequences of their delinquent actions.

I told them that I had talked to their parents, and the only consequences would be those dictated by their parents at home. This time they were quiet on the way back to their classroom. My bet is that they were wondering how quickly I had changed to a fair director, or better yet, a director who is fair!

Critical issues surrounding friendships and relationships:

- In general, females are neurobiologically predisposed to caring about relationships. That great chemical, oxytocin, known as the "tend and befriend" hormone, is part of the impetus.

- During childhood and adolescence, friendships take on an almost-as-important-as-oxygen essence.

- Girls will often have conflict and pain around relationships. As much as possible, adults need to let girls handle these occurrences and learn from them, with guidance only as needed.

- We need to help girls understand that they can be interdependent and independent without harming their important relationships. Often girls feel that they must be nice and agreeable to keep relationships smooth when expressing their own opinion and thoughts is an important part of relationship building.

The Big Five

The five big crucible events (discipline, risk-taking, change, loss/separation, and friendship) will probably happen to everyone at sometime in her/his life, regardless of age.

However, the above stories relate to young or preadolescent girls for a reason: these truly are the formative years, and early crucible events have a lifetime effect. There are many stories that could be told about older girls or women, but it is the events that occur up through adolescence that need to be underscored in terms of their impact on the developing human.

Crucible Moments

A crucible moment is more serendipitous, and to some extent, appears to be more trivial than a crucible event. However, as you have come to see, the layering over time with less-than-earth-shattering-moments makes up the substance of each person's strudel (whereas one could say that the crucible events are the filling!). These crucible moments lead to teachable moments: what happens afterwards; how they are responded to, dealt with, and discussed; all these help forge a person.

Examples of crucible events include such things as

- A roll of the eyes by the "queen bee" when you try to sit next to her in class.

- An off-hand comment by a teacher: "What is wrong with you?"

- Your dad saying to you: "Do you really need that cookie?"

Here's a moment in Liz's young life that will help us understand.

Liz was five, barely two-feet tall, with big blue eyes, still having some developmental troubles with her L's and R's, which had adults saying "Isn't she cute?" Liz was visiting her aunt in Ohio and had just arrived at my house, sans squirt gun, which she had been asked to bring.

In addition to Liz, also present was her nine-year-old brother (Steve), and three other boys (Adam, David, and Kevin), who were the children of another friend.

The play rules had been set for this ninety-degree July day. Everyone had a squirt gun and the gazebo, and only the gazebo, was the safe space. One step out of the gazebo and a person was an open target for being squirted. Liz, and her brother Steve, arrived late with their aunt. They all got out of the car and joined the adults who were sitting in the gazebo.

Liz stepped out of the gazebo before the rules were explained to her. She was promptly, systematically, and accurately squirted by all of the other kids. She screamed and ran back into the gazebo, making those heartbreaking child sobby noises. We are so programmed as caring adults to respond to the physical or emotional pain of small, living things, that it was not surprising that her Aunt Diana's response was to take Liz into her lap and wrap her arms around her. But her next action was surprising — she told Liz to come over and talk to me about what to do next.

Luckily, there was an unclaimed squirt gun on the table. I explained the rules of the squirt gun game, that the gazebo was a squirt free zone and outside of the gazebo was the squirt zone. "Liz," I said, "you can stay here in the gazebo and be unsquirted, or you can take the squirt gun and go back out into the yard with the other children." She opted for the squirt gun; I guess you can't always tell a book by its cover.

"Would you like me to fill the squirt gun with regular water or very cold water," I asked. "Very cold water," (and her lisp did add to her adorableness) was her answer. As she stepped out of the gazebo, she mumbled, "Prepare to die!" to no one in particular. The next screams were not from Liz.

Although neither of her parents were present for this crucible moment, it still illustrates how significant is the way parents and adults respond to the pain of a child in the forging of self.

Key factors in the handling of this crucible moment include:

- While acknowledging pain and providing a cuddly lap space is important, it is not enough, and if it is the only response, it can lead to forging a child who becomes weaker, not stronger.

- However, the nurturing response is certainly a critical and needed component. This reminds me to repeat again this basic tenet: a well-balanced blend of nurturing and challenging is the healthiest mix for the developing human — at any age. That's why I call it the Magic Blend.

- Choices, choices, choices. This concept cannot be stressed enough. It is up to the adult to help identify some choices, because the age, or life experiences, of children is not always such that they can see all of the viable choices. It is what my grandfather meant when he said, "Too late smart," referring to the wisdom accumulated over time with experience. In the above example, it would have been even better if Liz had been asked if she could think of any other alternatives.

The various components of confidence, competence, and connectedness in the above story should be quite apparent to the reader by now.

In all of the above examples, the adults involved made good choices, but the truth is, we make mistakes as adults in the lives of children and do not always behave or help children to behave so that wisdom and strength will be the end products. Nor can we control all of the other human beings in the world and how they will respond to the crucible moments or events in the life of any child, or to my child. Time for "insurance" policies!

Insurance Policies

Insurance policies are ways of buffering children who do not have perfect parents, perfect teachers, or perfect lives, from the trials and tribulations of life — which might forge them into unhealthy human beings, unlike those healthy children who have had every crucible moment or event handled perfectly!

An example of one kind of insurance policy is what Mary Pipher refers to as the "north star" in her book, *Reviving Ophelia*. A north star is something that a child has in her life that is precious, that she can count on, that she is passionate about. It might be the horse for the passionate rider, or the violin for the committed musician, or the hours spent on emailing or instant messaging with all those cyber-buddies. So that, as Mary Pipher says, when the waters get rough in adolescence and I come home from school knowing that I am a hope-less geek and that I will be the only one in the universe not going to my senior prom, I can go out to the stables and Mr. Ed still loves me. My north star, Mr. Ed, will be enough to hold me somewhat steady until a human "Mr. Ed" finally appreciates my worth.

One caveat is in order — parents cannot choose, or force a child to choose, a particular north star. Parents can only provide a rich smorgasbord early on in life and pray that a daughter finds her north star before her hormones kick into high gear.

Another insurance policy is what I call a green blanket. And since it's green, that must mean another story!

The Green Blanket

When I was in first grade, I thought a boy in the other first grade, Jay, was wonderful. We would get together at recess and play, sit together at lunch, and walk to the bus together after school. My mother called it puppy love, but I didn't think he looked like a puppy.

Well, sometime in the middle of the school year, this blonde girl moved into town and joined the first grade. Soon, Jay was playing with her, sitting by her at lunch, walking with her to the bus. It was like I didn't exist. My three C's took a big hit and I was miserable.

My mother came into my bedroom for "tuck-in time" that night. She covered me with the green blanket on my bed, touched my face, and said, "Honey, what's wrong?" "Jay doesn't like me any more!" I sobbed. "I must be ugly or stupid or something." My mother looked at me with what I call love lenses and she said what she truly believed, "But honey, you are the most beautiful first grader in the world." I slept well that night.

Girls who have an adult green blanket at home and an adult green blanket at school have an added insurance policy that holds them steadier when the waves start crashing against their boat. Friends at school are important, but having an adult whom you know is there for you is the icing on the cake.

If you look at the research and literature on resilience, there is another potential insurance policy lurking there. Researchers have looked at those children who didn't come into the world with high resilience (some do) but developed more emotional resilience and strength over time.

In trying to ferret out what could be the causes or enhancers or contributors to this growth, it was very difficult to isolate any single factor. However, one theme that was present: quantity of time spent with family. Quality time is certainly important, but quantity seems to be critical also. When families spend enough time being together, doing things together, talking, well, being a family in all of what that means, we see this protective effect permeating their lives.

Ending with a Beginning

This brings us to the end of the book. Of course, I hope the end also marks the beginning of a new relationship with the girls in our care. I hope all readers take away with them the clear understanding that gender inequities still exist, that our traditional methods of operating schools (and some kinds of parenting) have, and still do, contribute to these inequities.

I want us to examine the ways in which we may be working against the needs of girls, despite our best intentions, and strive towards solutions. And I want us to consciously focus on building and maintaining the self-esteem of girls in all of our interactions, knowing that in doing so we can help them realize their full potential. This, after all, is what we want — to clarify and act on the best practices in education and parenting that will allow all girls (and boys) to thrive in this world.

It is the hope of all educators and parents. And it is well within our grasp.

Stay Connected

If you have a story, a program or any thoughts that would add to our general knowledge of helping form a healthy and effective human being, please send me an email: jdeak@deakgroup.com. In return, I'll agree to be your email green blanket if you ever need to "talk" to anyone.

Resources for Parents and Educators
Books/Articles/Reports*

*American Girl, ed. *Raising an American Girl: Parenting Advice for the Real World*. American Girl Publishing Co, March, 2010. N.B. Includes a chapter by Dr. JoAnn Deak.

*Barnoski, Robert. *Preliminary Findings for the Juvenile Rehabilitation Administration's Mentoring Program*. Washington State Institute for Public Policy, 2002.

*Beaman, Robyn et al. "Differential Teacher Attention to Boys and Girls in the Classroom." *Educational Review*, Vol. 58, No. 3, August.

*Beery, K.E. and Buktenica, N.A. *Beery-Buktenica Developmental Test of Visual-Motor Integration 5th Edition*. Multi-Health Systems, Incorporated, 2006.

*Belenky, Mary et al. *Women's Ways of Knowing*. Basic Books, 1997.

*Benson, Peter L., et al. *What Kids Need to Succeed*. Free Spirit Publishing, 1998.

Beyond the Gender Wars: A Conversation About Girls, Boys, and Education. American Association of University Women, 2001.

Blais, Madeleine. *In These Girls Hope is a Muscle*. Grand Central Publishing, 1996.

Bloom, Floyd E., MD. *Best of the Brain from Scientific American*. Dana Press, 2007.

Borba, Dr. Michele. *Esteem Builders: A K-8 Self Esteem Curriculum for Improving Student Achievement, Behavior and School Climate,* second edition. Jalmar Press, 2003.

*Bridges, William. *Managing Transitions: Making the most of Change*, 2nd edition. Da Capo Press, 2003.

*Brizendine, Louann. *The Female Brain*. Broadway Books, 2006.

Bronson, Po and Merryman, Ashley. *Nurture Shock, New Thinking About Children*. Hatchette Book Group, 2009.

Brown, Lyn Mikel. *Girl Fighting: Betrayal and Rejection Among Girls*. University Press, 2005.

*Brown, Lyn Mikel, *Meeting at the Crossroad*. Diane Publishing Co., 1998.

*Cahill, Larry. "His Brain, Her Brain." *Scientific American*, May 2005.

Carper, Jean. *Your Miracle Brain: Maximize Your Brain Power, Boost Your Memory, Lift Your Mood, Improve Your IQ, Prevent and Reverse Mental Aging*. Quill Books, 1999.

Carter, Rita. *The Human Brain Book*. DK Publishing, New York. 2009.

Ceci, Stephen J. *The Mathematics of Sex: How Biology and Society Conspire to Limit Talented Girls and Women*. Oxford University Press, 2009.

Cahill, Larry. "His Brain, Her Brain." *Scientific American*, May 2005.

*Chadwell, David. "South Carolina: Lessons from Two Years of a State Initiative." *Advances in Gender and Education*, 1, 2009.

*Item is referenced in the text of *How Girls Thrive*

*Coghlan, Andy. "Gay Brains Structured Like Those of the Opposite Sex." *New Scientist,* June 2008.

Countryman, Joan. *Writing to Learn Mathematics: Strategies That Work, K-12.* Heinemann, 1992.

Darlington, Cynthia. *The Female Brain,* 2nd edition. CRC Press, 2009.

Datnow, Amanda and Hubbard, Lea eds. *Gender in Policy and Practice: Perspectives on Single Sex and Coeducational Schooling.* Routledge, 2002.

*Deak, JoAnn. *Girls Will Be Girls: Raising Confident and Courageous Daughters.* Hyerion, 2002.

Deak, JoAnn. "Moral and Character Development: Making a Difference in Girl's Lives." *Connections,* Vol. XXIX, No. 7, May 2010.

DeBare, Ilana. *Where Girls Come First: The Rise, Fall and Surprising Revival of Girls' Schools.* Penguin, 2005.

*Drake, Elizabeth and Barnoski, Robert. *Recidivism Findings for the Juvenile Rehabilitation Administration's Mentoring Program: Final Report.* Washington State Institute for Public Policy, 2006.

DuBois, David L. and Silverthorn, Naida. "National Mentoring Relationships and Adolescent Health: Evidence form a National Study." *American Journal of Public Health.* V. 95, No. 3, March 2005.

*Duncan, Annette and Schmidt, Amy. "Building Sisterhood and Brotherhood in Gender-Specific Classrooms." *Advances in Gender and Education,* 1, 2009.

Dweck, Carol, *Mindset: The New Psychology of Success.* Random House, 2006.

Early Implementation of Public Single-Sex Schools: Perceptions and Characteristics. U.S. Department of Education, 2008.

Eliot, Lise. *Pink Brain, Blue Brain: How Small Differences Grow Into Troublesome Gaps -- And What We Can Do About It.* Houghton Mifflin Harcourt, 2009.

Exploring Girls Leadership, Girl Scout Research Institute, 2007.

*Fennema, Elizabeth and Leder, Gilah C. *Mathematics and Gender.* Teacher's College Press, 1990.

*Ferrara, Margaret M. "The Student and the Teacher — Making a Match in a Single-Gender Classroom." *Advances in Gender and Education,* 1, 2009.

*Flansburg, Sundra Cee. *Building Self: Adolescent Girls and Self-Esteem.* Education Development Center, 2001.

*Francis, Becky. *Reassessing Gender and Achievement: Questioning Contemporary Key Issues.* Routledge, 2005.

*Gardner, Howard. *Five Minds for the Future.* Harvard Business School Press, 2007.

Gladwell, Malcolm. *Blink: The Power of Thinking Without Thinking.* Little, Brown and Company, 2005.

Gladwell, Malcolm. *The Tipping Point: How Little Things Can Make a Big Difference.* Little, Brown and Company, 2000.

Galdwell, Malcolm. *Outliers: The Story of Success*. Little, Brown and Company, 2008.

Gilles, Robyn M. *Cooperative Learning: Integrating Theory and Practice*. Sage Publications, Inc., 2009.

*Gilligan, Carol. *In a Different Voice*. Harvard University Press, 1993.

*Gurian, Michael. *Successful Single Sex Classrooms*. Jossey-Bass, 2009.

*Hafner, Katie. "Texting May Be Taking a Toll." *New York Times*, May 25, 2009.

*Herrera, Carla et al, *Making a Difference in Schools: The Big Brothers Big Sisters School-Based Mentoring Impact Study*. Public/Orivate Ventures, 2007.

Honnold, Rosemary. *More Teen Programs That Work*. Neal-Schuman Publishers, Inc., 2005.

Horstman, Judith. *The Scientific American Day in the Life of your Brain*. Jossey-Bass Publishing Co., 2009.

How Schools Shortchange Girls. American Association of University Women, 1992.

Jacobs, Dr. George M. *Teacher's Sourcebook for Cooperative Learning: Practical Techniques, Basic Principles, and Frequently Asked Questions*. Corwin Press, 2002.

Johnson, David W. *Cooperative Learning in the Classroom*. Association for Supervision and Curriculum Development Deve, 1994.

Karres, Erika V. Shearin and Rutledge, Rebecca. *The Everything Parent's Guide to Raising Girls: A Complete Handbook to Develop Confidence, Promote Self-Esteem and Improve Communication*. F+W Publications, Inc., 2007.

Kelly, Joe. *Dads and Daughters: How to Inspire, Understand and Support Your Daughter When She's Growing Up So Fast*. Broadway Books, 2002.

*Kimura, Doreen. *Sex and Cognition*. The MIT Press, 2000.

*Krupnick, Catherine G. "Women and Men in the Classroom: Inequality and Its Remedies." *On Teaching and Learning*, Vol. 1, 1985.

Laster, Madlon T. *Teach the Way the Brain Learns: Curriculum Themes Build Neuron Networks*. Rowman & Littlefield Education, 2009.

Laster, Madlon T. *Brain-Based Teaching for All Subjects: Patterns to Promote Learning*. Rowman & Littlefield Education, 2007.

*Leinwand, Donna. "Survey: 1 in 5 Teens 'Sext' Despite Risks." *USA Today*, June 25, 2009.

Lewin, Tamar. "Bias Called Persistent Hurdle for Women in Sciences." *New York Times*, March 22, 2010.

*Lewin, Tama. "Teenage Insults Scrawled on Web, Not on Walls." *New York Times*, May 5, 2010.

Long-Term Effects of a Middle School Engineering Outreach Program for Girls: A Controlled Study. American Society for Engineering Education, 2007.

McCarthy, Moira. *Everything Guide to Raising Adolescent Girls*. F+W Publications, Inc., 2008.

*Manegold, Catherine S. "Gains Aside, Bill Seeks Equality of Sexes in School." *New York Times*, February 13, 1994.

*Marano, Hara Estroff. "Big Bad Bully." *Psychology Today*, September 1, 1995.

Meehan, Diana. *Learning Like a Girl: Educating Our Daughters in Schools of Their Own*. PublicAffairs, 2007.

Meeker, Meg. *Strong Fathers, Strong Daughters: 10 Secrets Every Father Should Know*. Ballantine Books, 2007.

Michels, Michael. *Cooperative Learning and Science: High School Activities*. Kagan Cooperative Learning, 2003.

Miller, Carol L. *Mentoring Teens: A Resource Guide*. BookSurge Publishing, 2006.

*Miller, Claire Cain. "Barbie's Next Career? Computer Engineer." *New York Times*, February 12, 2010.

Mogel, Wendy, *The Blessing of a Skinned Knee*. Scribner; Reprint edition, 2008.

*Myhill, Debra. "Bad Boys and Good Girls? Patterns of Interaction and Response in Whole Class Teaching." *British Educational Research Journal*, Vol. 28, No. 3, 2002.

*"Napping Can Prime the Brain for Learning." *New York Times*, February 23, 2010.

* "The New Science of the Brain — Why Men and Women Think Differently." *Newsweek*, March 27, 1995.

*Paretsky, Sara. "How Sports Can Change a Girl's Life." *Parade*, April 25, 2010.

Partridge, Kenneth, ed. *The Brain*. HW Wilson Company, New York, 2009.

Paul, Dierdre Glenn. *Talkin' Back: Raising and Educating Resiliant Black Girls*. Praeger Publishers, 2003.

*Pink, Daniel. *A Whole New Mind: Why Right Brains Will Rule the Future*. New York. Riverhead Books, 2006.

*Pipher, Mary. *Reviving Ophelia: Saving the Selves of Adolescent Girls*. Riverhead Trade, 2005.

Preuschoff, Gisela. *Raising Girls: Why Girls are Different and How to Help Them Grow Up Happy and Strong*. Celestial Arts, 2006.

Probst, Kristie. *Mentoring for Meaningful Results: Asset-Building Tips, Tools, and Activities for Youth and Adults*. Search Institute Press, 2006.

Protheroe, Nancy. "Single-Sex Classrooms." *Principal*, May/June, 2009.

Real Girls, Real Pressure: A National Report on Self-Esteem. Dove Self-Esteem Fund, 2008.

Rhodes, Jean E. *Stand by Me: The Risks and Rewards of Mentoring Today's Youth*. Harvard University Press, 2004.

Robinson-English, Tracey. "Saving Black Boys: Is Single-Sex Education the Answer?" *Ebony*, December, 2006.

*Sadker, David and Nancy. *Failing at Fairness: How Our Schools Cheat Girls*. Sribner, 1995.

*Sadker, Nancy and Frazier, Myra. *Sexism and Society*. Harper, 1973.

Salomone, Professor Rosemary C. *Same, Different, Equal: Rethinking Single-Sex Schooling*. Yale University, 2003.

*Sax, Linda J. *Women Graduates of Single-Sex and Coeducational High Schools: Differences in Their Characteristics and the Transition to College*. UCLA Graduate School of Education & Information Studies, 2009.

Schwarz, Patrick and Kluth, Paula. *You're Welcome: 30 Innovative Ideas for the Inclusive Classroom*. Heinemann, 2007.

Scientific American Mind, May 2010. Special issue "His Brain, Her Brain: How We're Different."

Sheehy, Sandy. *Connecting; The Enduring Power of Female Friendship*. William Morrow, 2000.

Shortchanging Girls, Shortchanging America. American Association of University Women, 1991.

Simpson, Kathleen. *The Human Brain: Inside Your Body's Control Room*. National Geographic, 2009.

Stiles, Joan. *The Fundamentals of Brain Development: Integrating Nature and Nurture*. Harvard University Press, 2008.

Stout, Hilary. "Antisocial Networking?" *New York Times*, April 30, 2010.

The Supergirl Dilemma: Girls Grappling with the Mounting Pressure of Expectations. Girls Incorporated, 2006.

Sweeny, Michael S. *Brain, The Complete Mind: How it Develops, How it Works and How to Keep it Sharp*. National Geographic, 2009.

Tannen, Deborah. *You Just Don't Understand: Women and Men in Conversation*. Harper Paperbacks, 2001.

Tech Savvy: Educating Girls in the New Computer Age. American Association of University Women, 2000.

Teens and Mobile Phones. Pew Internet and American Life Project, 2010.

Thurber, James. *Many Moons*. Sandpiper, 1998.

Toppo, Greg. "Single-Sex School Restrictions Ease." *USA Today*, October 25, 2006.

Trends in Educational Equity of Girls & Women 2004. National Center for Education Statistics, 2004.

Trevathan, Melissa and Goff, Sissy. *Raising Girls*. Zondervan, 2007.

Tyler, Marya Washington. *On-the-Job Math Mysteries*. Prufrock Press, Inc., October 2008.

Udvari-Solner, Alice and Kluth, Paula M. *Joyful Learning: Active and Collaborative Learning in Inclusive Classrooms*. Corwin Press, 2007.

Under the Microscope: A Decade of Gender Equity Projects in the Sciences. American Association of University Women, 2004.

*_Where the Girls Are: The Facts About Gender Equity in Education._ American Association of University Women, 2008.

*_Why So Few?_ American Association of University Women, 2010.

*Williams, Alex. "The New Math on Campus." _New York Times,_ February 7, 2010.

Willis, Judy. _Inspiring Middle School Minds: Gifted, Creative, And Challenging._ Great Potential Press, 2009.

Zaslow, Jeffrey. "The Ties That Bind." _Wall Street Journal,_ May 16, 2009.

Zaslow, Jeffrey. _The Girls From Ames: A Story of Women & a Forty-Year Friendship._ Gotham, 2009.

Websites

*American Association of University Women: www.aauw.org

*Association for School Curriculum Development (now known as ASCD): www.ascd.org

Association for Women in Mathematics Mentor Network: www.awm-math.org/mentornetwork.html

Association for Women in Science: www.awis.org

*Big Brothers Big Sisters: www.bbbs.org

*Bunting-Cobb Residence Hall: www.rci.rutgers.edu/~dougproj/programs/BC/info.html

Center for Research on Girls at Laurel School: www.laurelschool.org/about/CRGat-Laurel.cfm

Collaborative for Gender Equity: www.genderequitycollaborative.org

*Community Action Commission (sponsors Across Ages mentoring program): www.virtualcap.org

Dana Foundation: www.dana.org

The Deak Group: www.deakgroup.com

Education Northwest National Mentoring Center: http://educationnorthwest.org/nmc

Engineer Your Life (A guide to engineering for high school girls): www.engineeryourlife.org

*Everyday Mathematics: http://everydaymath.uchicago.edu/

Eyes to the Future (Middle School Girls Envisioning Science and Technology in High School and Beyond): http://etf.terc.edu/index.html

*Girl Scouts of the U.S.A.: www.girlscouts.org

Girl Zone: www.girlzone.com

Girls' Angle (a math club for girls): www.girlsangle.org

*Girls Can Do Anything magazine: www.gcdamagazine.com

*Girls Inc.: www.girlsinc.org

Girls on the Run: www.girlsrun.org

Hardy Girls Healthy Women: www.hardygirlshealthywomen.org (check their resources page)

Icouldbe.org (an e-mentoring site): www.icouldbe.org

Inspiring Girls Now in Technology Evolution: www.ignite-us.org

Institute of Education Sciences: http://ies.ed.gov

Kagan Cooperative Learning: www.kaganonline.com

*Madeira School Co-Curriculum: www.madeira.org/on-campus/co-curriculum/index.aspx

*Mathematical Association of America Women and Mathematics Network: www.maa.org/wam/

Mentor: www.mentoring.org

Mentor Consulting Group: www.Mentorconsultinggroup.com

MIT STEM Program: http://web.mit.edu/stem/About.html

Montgomery Center for Research in Child and Adolescent Development: www.mcrcad.org

* National Association for the Education of Young Children: www.naeyc.org

*National Association for Single Sex Public Education: www.singlesexschools.org

National Center for Education Statistics: http://nces.ed.gov

*National Coalition of Girls Schools: www.ncgs.org

*National Council for Teachers of Mathematics: www.nctm.org

National Education Association: www.nea.org

National Women's Law Center (Gender Equity in Education): www.nwlc.org

Neuroscience for kids: http://faculty.washington.edu/chudler/neurok.html

New Moon Girls: www.newmoon.com

*Pace Center for Girls: www.pacecenter.org

*Pew Internet and American Life Project: www.pewinternet.org

*Power Play NYC: www.powerplaynyc.org/stars.php

*Project Implicit: https://implicit.harvard.edu/implicit/

Science Club for Girls: www.scienceclubforgirls.org

SciGirls: http://pbskids.org/scigirls/

*Take Our Daughters and Sons to Work Foundation: www.daughtersandsonstowork.org

*Tarrant County Challenge, Inc.: www.tcchallenge.org

TED Ideas Worth Spreading: www.ted.com (talks by Malcolm Gladwell, and by Rebecca Saxe)

Under the Microscope where women and science connect: www.underthemicroscope.com

*U.S. Department of Education: www.ed.gov

U.S. Department of Education Mentoring Resource Center: www.edmentoring.org

*Wellesley Centers for Women: www.wcwonline.org

Women in Engineering Proactive Network: http://wepan.affiniscape.com

*Women in Science and Engineering at Duke University: www.duke.edu/web/wise/programs.html

*Write Girl: www.writegirl.org

About The Authors

JoAnn Deak, Ph.D., has spent more than thirty years as an educator and psychologist, helping children develop into confident and competent adults, as well as instructing and encouraging adults, parents and teachers in their roles as guides or "neurosculptors" of children. She has a doctorate in Preventive Psychology, participated in Carol Gilligan's ground-breaking study on girls, and consults with parents, schools, and other organizations nationwide and internationally. Dr. Deak has been awarded the Woman of Achievement Award by the National Coalition of Girls' Schools, was given the first Female Educator of the Year Award by Orchard House School, and the Outstanding Partner for Girls Award from Clemson University. She has been named the Visiting Scholar in New Zealand, the Visiting Scholar for Montessori Children's House, and has been the Resident Scholar for the Gardner Carney Leadership Institute in Colorado Springs for the past five years.

In addition to writing numerous articles and contributions to other books, Dr Deak has also written *Girls Will Be Girls: Raising Confident and Courageous Daughters*, Hyperion, 2002.

She is currently at work on a series of books: *Brainology 101 for Students/Teachers/Parents*.

www.deakgroup.com
jdeak@deakgroup.com

Dory Adams has spent almost her entire life in education first as a student, then librarian, and then director of development; finally, working at the National Association of Independent Schools on professional development for teachers and administrators, and on gender equity for girls and women. Taking all that she had learned, she applied it to consulting with schools, and helping individuals as an Executive/Career/Life Coach for 7 years before marrying, moving to Gettysburg, Pennslyvania, and settling down in a 1790s stone house with husband, Denny, Airedale, Jack, and rumored ghosts. This is her first book, but she hopes, not her last.

Dornie46@gmail.com